the
e-marketing
handbook

the e-marketing handbook

**An Indispensable
Guide to Marketing**

Your Products
and Services on
the Internet

matt haig

KOGAN
PAGE

First published in 2001

Kogan Page Limited
120 Pentonville Road
London
N1 9JN
UK

Kogan Page Limited
163 Central Avenue, Suite 2
Dover
NH 03820
USA

British Library Cataloguing in Publication Data

A CIP record for this book is available from the British Library.

ISBN 0 7494 3547 X

Typeset by Saxon Graphics Ltd, Derby
Printed and bound by Creative Print and Design (Wales) Ebbw Vale

contents

Contents _____

List of figures

Introduction

The Internet is not just a new form of medium. It brings with it an entirely new kind of marketing, not only changing the nature of a business and its market, but also transforming the way they relate to each other.

Although the term 'Internet revolution' has already become somewhat misleading, the Internet's potential to revolutionize marketing practice is now undeniable. As a result, practically every long-established 'real world' business now also has a very strong presence on the Web, and many have even shifted their entire operation online. The secret is out. Cyberspace is now considered too important a place to be left to the Internet start-ups.

Although marketers have taken their heads out of the sand to recognize the importance of the Internet as a marketing tool, there remains a considerable degree of uncertainty over how exactly it should be used. However, one clear consensus of opinion is emerging. E-marketing is about more than state-of-the-art Web sites and search engine rankings: it is about using the Internet to listen and respond to the needs of your market to an extent previously considered impossible.

New media, new marketing

As the rest of this book will show, the Internet does not just represent a new technology, it also opens up a whole new way of marketing the products and services you have to offer. The secret to succeeding on the Internet is therefore to understand how e-marketing differs from traditional marketing practice. By appreciating what these differences are, you will be able to disregard the old marketing rule book and start thinking from an e-marketing perspective. Here are some of the key characteristics of this new media marketing.

Pull over push

The Internet is a 'pull' rather than 'push' medium. This means Internet users pull the information they want towards them. There is no effective way to push your business message in front of people who haven't asked to hear it. This is why 'spamming' (the act of sending unsolicited junk e-mail) is considered to be the ultimate e-marketing *faux pas*.

Disintermediation

One of the most radical effects of the Internet is what e-marketers refer to as *disintermediation*. This basically means the end of the intermediary, or the middleman. For instance, a business can now get its message across directly, without relying on journalists or editors.

Audiences of one

Whereas traditional media *broad*cast the same message to a mass audience, the Internet *narrow*casts messages to individuals. The Internet's raison d'être is choice: by using powerful search engine technology net surfers can pick out exactly the material they want from millions of Web pages. In a world of niche markets and even smaller population segments, the Internet therefore has the potential to become the ultimate communication tool enabling you to target 'audiences of one'.

Speed marketing

The Internet is reckoned to travel at seven times the speed of normal time. People often visit the same Web site many times in one week. Companies therefore need to make every effort to make sure that their Web site content is fresh and up to date. Another consequence of the Internet's fast pace is that people expect e-mail messages to be responded to within 24 hours.

The word of Web

Related to speed marketing is the fast moving 'word of Web'. Whereas in the real world word of mouth publicity (whether good or bad) can take time to build, on the Internet (as we shall see later in this book) word of Web spreads almost instantaneously across networked markets.

Polarization

The Internet has a tendency to polarize markets. A few years ago it was thought that niche marketing was more suited to the Internet than mass marketing. The success of companies such as Yahoo!, AOL and Amazon, however, has shown this is not the case. On the Internet niche *and* mass markets can thrive, albeit at the expense of the middle market. To succeed online, companies therefore either have to fine tune their product range to cater for a strong but narrow market, or broaden it to offer a complete 'one stop shop'. This has led to the new marketing motto, 'diversify or die'.

Increased competition

No matter how 'niche' your online enterprise is, the chances are there are other people out there doing something similar. The Internet may have made the world a smaller place, but it has made the market a whole lot bigger. You therefore need to add value to your Web site, and differentiate your online business from its competition.

Intimacy

Although the Internet is often viewed as an impersonal medium, it actually allows businesses to get closer to their customers than ever before. As Kevin Roberts, CEO for Saatchi and Saatchi Worldwide, says, 'People open up and share how they feel on the net – something they just don't do in more classical research formats such as focus groups.'

Market knowledge

The Internet enables you to find out more information on your customers and competition than ever before. By the same token, they can also find out more about your business. The convenience of e-mail and the accessibility of Web sites mean that everyone is less likely to be kept in the dark.

Marketing from the outside in

E-marketing experts generally agree that the secret to online success is marketing from the outside in. This means that instead of starting with what you do and how you do it, you have to start with what the customer wants.

E-marketing and the four Ps

Marketing is often divided up into what marketers refer to as 'the four Ps': Product, Price, Place and Promotion. To understand the full significance of the Internet in this context, it is therefore useful to reassess the four Ps in terms of e-marketing.

Product

Online marketers have to think of various new factors in relation to the products they sell. One of the most obvious is the fact that customers cannot see or touch products in the same way they can in the real world. This explains why products such as books, CDs and computer goods have traditionally fared better than food and clothes. Another even more significant factor to be considered is how to integrate products with useful content. Many Internet experts talk of the 'information product' when thinking of ways to increase product value by offering relevant and exclusive information.

Price

There are many instances online where the Internet places a downward pressure on prices. The Internet increases the chances for comparative shopping and even in some cases (such as at Priceline.com) enables customers to set their own prices. Another thing to take into consideration is that buying lower priced goods involves minimal risk on the part of Internet users and will therefore encourage them to make their first purchase at a Web site. However, although pricing is an important factor in getting users to buy products online, it is by no means the only one. Sites that encourage useful information and two-way interaction are likely to attract customers even if their prices aren't the lowest.

Place

In the real world, location is often seen as the all important marketing factor. If your shop is conveniently located or your office has a prestigious address, it can certainly have an impact on your marketing success rate. On the Internet, on the other hand, your real world business location becomes almost irrelevant. Wherever you set up you will be able to reach people around the world. Although geographical limitations are practically eliminated, cultural differences remain. For instance, if you are targeting an international audience you will need to think about different language options and currency converters for your site (see Chapter 1).

Promotion

The Internet puts the promotion of your business on your own terms. Rather than relying on advertising or journalists to get your message across, you can communicate directly with your audience. As the Internet is a 'pull' rather than 'push' medium, paid advertising is often not as effective as free marketing methods such as search engine submissions and discussion group contributions. One of the most powerful forms of online promotion is word of mouth, referred to as 'viral marketing'. As Internet markets are networked, positive (and negative) publicity can spread with incredible speed. This means the promotional message must always be in tune with, and preferably incorporate, the voice of the market.

About this book

This book is intended to provide you with the background knowledge and practical advice necessary to succeed as an Internet marketer. The differences between online and offline marketing are highlighted, as are the emerging points of contact between the two disciplines. This *E-marketing Handbook* also seeks to explore some of the more radical ways the Internet is revolutionizing marketing practice and turning it, perhaps surprisingly, into a thoroughly more *human* discipline.

More specifically, this book will help you:

- improve your market knowledge;
- design a user-friendly Web site;
- build two-way relations between your site and its audience;
- use search engines as a marketing tool;
- seek partnerships with other Web sites;
- develop an e-mail strategy;
- create and distribute e-newsletters;
- convert passive visitors into active customers;
- provide ongoing customer support;
- build an e-brand;
- look at the pros and cons of online advertising;
- seek free media coverage for your site;
- integrate your online and offline marketing activity;
- measure and evaluate results.

In addition, this book's aim is to help you make the transition towards a more inclusive form of marketing based around information and interaction, in which the customer is involved at every level.

one

Getting **focused**

The Internet is, in many ways, the most effective marketing tool that has ever existed. It enables businesses to interact with their market to an extent previously unwitnessed. Companies and consumers can find out more about each other than ever before and engage in the sort of two-way relationships unimaginable in the 'era of production' (as marketing academics tend to call the pre-Internet Industrial Age).

However, while the Internet can help eliminate the guesswork involved in finding out what the customer wants, it cannot tell you what your own objectives should be. This chapter therefore looks at the various things you need to consider before embarking online in order for you to add focus to your Internet activity, as well as to prevent you getting lost in the e-marketing maze.

Planning your e-marketing activity

The exact nature of your e-marketing activity will depend on the following things:

- *What* you want to achieve.
- *How* you are going to achieve it.
- *When* you want to achieve it by.
- *Who* is responsible for different tasks.
- *How much* you are prepared to spend.

These factors, taken collectively, will help you plan your e-marketing campaign and will form the background for your objectives. Furthermore, they will help you, when setting these objectives to ensure that they are SMART – that is to say Specific, Measurable, Achievable, Realistic and Timetabled:

- *Specific*. When you are planning online business and marketing activity you need to be as specific as you possibly can. A vague objective such as, 'To satisfy the needs of my online audience' is clearly unhelpful. To turn this into a specific objective you would have to define 'audience', 'needs' and 'satisfaction' in this context.
- *Measurable*. If it is impossible to measure the objectives you have set yourself in an e-marketing plan it will be difficult to know whether you are on course or not. Fortunately, as shall be revealed later on in this book, the Internet's self-documenting nature enables the marketer to monitor and track results to a greater extent than ever before.
- *Achievable*. There is little point in setting objectives that cannot be achieved. By taking the time to understand your market and by analysing your current situation you will be able to distinguish between what is achievable and what is not.
- *Realistic*. To achieve your objectives you need to be realistic about the capabilities of your business. Factors such as budget, manpower and Internet experience must be taken into consideration.
- *Timetabled*. Setting completion dates for activities will help you structure your marketing efforts. When you are putting together a timetable for your online marketing campaigns you need to remember that the e-business world moves a lot faster than the offline business environment.

It is important that, however you decide to put your plan together, you are willing to adjust and adapt it according to any unforeseen changes affecting your business or market.

The other thing to remember when putting a plan together is to think from the perspective of your customers, because ultimately the success of your e-marketing activity hinges on how well it is received by your online audience. Of course, this is not always easy. In fact in some cases your objectives might seem diametrically opposed to those of your online audience (for instance, your main objective could be 'to make x amount of money' while a typical audience objective is 'to save money'). However, you should try to concentrate on the areas where both sets of objectives overlap so that in working for your own best interests you are also helping to enrich your customer's online experience.

E-marketing strategies

When you are planning your e-marketing campaign you will need to think very carefully about the strategies you are going to use to reach your objectives. Although your Web site will inevitably be at the centre of all your online activity, it is important to realize that it is not the only way to achieve your marketing goals. As well as Web sites, online marketers have the following tools at their disposal:

- *E-mail*. E-mail was the first Internet application and remains the most widely used. It can be strategically employed for direct marketing purposes, as well as for communicating on a one-to-one basis with members of your target audience.
- *Newsletters*. Electronic newsletters should be considered when you are working out your e-marketing strategy, as they provide a way of keeping the site-visitor relationship alive for the long term.
- *Discussion groups*. Web-based discussion groups are an integral part of the e-marketing mix, as they provide a means of reaching and researching key members of your target audience. Furthermore, it is important to monitor these online groups in order to prevent misinformation spreading about your business.

When you are planning your e-marketing strategy it is important not to view any of these tools in isolation. For example, you can promote your e-mail newsletter on your Web site, and vice versa. Combining different Internet tools within one strategy can improve your chances of success, ensuring your online activity becomes as comprehensive as possible.

In addition to thinking of the diverse range of tools you can use, it is also helpful to think of the two main reasons people decide to go onto the Internet: information and interaction.

Information. As most people who use the Internet do so to find information, you need to think of the ways in which you can provide your audience with relevant and useful information. When you are planning an e-marketing strategy you need to think about not only how to supply the kind of information your customers are after, but also how to find out information about your market, so you will have more to go on when implementing your strategy.

Interaction. The Internet is an interactive medium mainly used for communication. Although e-mail is the most popular means of online communication, chat rooms, discussion groups and Web sites can also be used to encourage a two-way dialogue between your business and its online audience. As one of the e-marketer's primary aims is to increase the 'lifetime value' of each online customer, it is important for the long term to establish and consolidate meaningful and mutually beneficial site-visitor relations. In the real world this is rarely possible as traditional marketing methods confine the involvement of the audience to that of passive spectator.

Although increasing numbers of people are using the Internet to purchase products or services, it is not enough simply to use a Web site as a crude sales vehicle such as a catalogue or brochure. If your e-marketing strategy is to display and sell products and nothing else, you will only be able to compete on price. As we have already discovered, Internet users can conduct comparative shopping searches to find the cheapest products available, without an real difficulty. Unless you are willing to operate with zero profit margins, there is always likely to be a cheaper alternative. To avoid falling into this price trap, you need to think of ways to offer valuable information and interaction as part of your e-marketing strategy. As with online objectives, the success of your strategy depends on your ability to match your own aims and interests with those of your audience.

Identifying your online audience

One of the most important questions any business, either online or offline, must ask is, 'Who are we targeting?' Without being able to accurately identify your audience, your marketing efforts are going to be at best misguided, and often counterproductive. On the Internet, audience identification is especially important for the following reasons:

- *The 'pull' factor.* In cyberspace there is no such thing as passing trade. Internet users must take the effort to 'pull' your site towards them, if they are to see what your business has to offer. This means that your site must appeal to their specific needs or requirements to a greater extent than, say, a high street shop.

■ *Niche markets*. Owing to the absence of any geographical constraints, on the Internet people become grouped around areas of interest. Internet users interested in, say, a certain type of music can visit sites and join discussion groups that relate solely to that particular type of music. Unless you have the marketing power of the major portal sites such as Yahoo! and AOL, which can group diverse online communities together, it can be very difficult to become all things to all people. For small and medium-sized businesses it is much more cost-effective to concentrate on one clearly defined niche audience than to try to cast the broadest net possible.

■ *Increased competition*. It is likely that your business will have more competitors online than it would in the real world. A clear knowledge of your target audience will help you to differentiate your online activity from that of your competition.

■ *International audience*. As people will be able to access your Web site from anywhere in the world, it is important to identify which international audiences you are targeting. After all, although the Internet makes the world a smaller place, cultural differences remain and should be recognized.

Although your target audience should be as clearly defined as possible, it is likely that you will want your online marketing action to reach more than one specific group of people. For instance, if your business is aimed at consumers you may have different product ranges aimed at completely different customers. If this is the case, you should try to divide your audience into as many different 'microsegments' as possible. Once you have done this you then have two options. You can either decide to cater for all of these audiences simultaneously or you can prioritize those audiences that are most important for your site. In other words, you should plan your e-marketing strategy with your main, clearly defined audience in mind and put together different parallel strategies for several target groups.

E-marketers can cater for different audiences at the same time in a number of ways. These include:

■ *Multiple Web sites*. If your products appeal to different audiences, you could set up a site for each individual product range.

■ *Different e-mail boxes*. Different e-mail addresses can be set up to cater for individual audiences. This is particularly useful if you intend to set up an automated e-mail response system.

- *Segmented sites.* It is possible to cater for diverse groups of people by dividing your site into segments based on each group's interest. Each different area can then be clearly identified on the home page.
- *Language options.* If you are targeting international audiences you should seriously consider providing different language options (see Figure 1.1) as well as currency converters.

The other point you need to consider is that on the Internet your audience does not just consist of customers; there are many other people who can affect the success of your e-marketing activity. These may include (take a deep breath): search engine review staff, discussion group moderators, online regulators, sponsors, job-seekers, advertisers, interest groups, consumer activists, journalists, competitors, investors, industry pundits, online affiliates and last but by no means least, employees.

Once your site has been placed on the Web it is there for anyone interested in your business to take a look at. It is therefore important

Figure 1.1 APC Web site. The online fashion retailer APC provides different language options for its international audience

when you come to design your site to think about the people beyond your immediate target audience who will be interested, for whatever reason, in what your site has to say.

Getting equipped

If you are setting up an e-business from scratch or if you are planning to create the first Web site for your offline business, you will need to consider the equipment required. Although the Internet has liberated business from various financial and geographical constraints, it hasn't (quite) obliterated start-up costs. To carry out e-marketing activity there are certain unavoidables in terms of computer hardware and software.

A computer

When choosing a computer the main thing marketers need to consider is the computer's power. For e-marketing purposes you will need a fast computer with a lot of Random Access Memory (RAM). The more RAM a computer has, the better, as it will mean your computer will be able to work quicker and support more data, as well as being more reliable. Ideally, you should have a computer with at least 128MB of RAM.

It isn't really that important whether you have a Mac or a PC as most software packages are now compatible on both types of computer.

A connection

To connect to the Internet you will need a special piece of hardware referred to as a modem. The word 'modem' is a hybrid of MOdulate/DEModulate, which refers to the technical process of Internet connection. Nowadays computers are often already equipped with internal modems, although you can still buy external ones.

A modem uses a phone line to make an Internet connection. While a standard phone line is more than adequate for personal purposes, for e-marketing activity it is better to use an upgraded phone line that ensures a faster and more powerful connection.

Ideally you should use a phone line that depends on ADSL (Asymmetric Digital Subscriber Line) technology, as ADSL lines ensure instant Internet access. Of course, if you are a large business with computers connected to a local area network your Internet access will usually be constant.

Software

There are various pieces of software that may prove useful or, in some cases, essential to your e-marketing activity.

A *Web browser* is probably the most vital, as it enables you to browse the WWW and download relevant material. Without it your computer will not be able to display Web pages. Microsoft Internet Explorer and Netscape Navigator are by far the most widely used browsers, and one of them is likely to come as part of your computer package or through your ISP (Internet Service Provider).

Alongside a Web browser, you will also need to get hold of *e-mail software*. While most ISPs will be able to provide you with e-mail software free of charge, generally these free programs are illsuited for marketing purposes, especially if you are likely to send and receive substantial quantities of e-mail. It will probably be more beneficial to seek out more sophisticated e-mail programs such as Microsoft's Outlook Express or Eudora Pro.

In addition to a browser and e-mail software you may also require *web design* and *shopping-cart software*, both of which are discussed in more detail elsewhere in this book.

An ISP

An ISP provides you with the software needed for your modem to dial and connect to the Internet. There are literally thousands of ISPs out there and choosing the right one can take some time.

Prior to choosing an ISP, you will need to know how reliable they are, how quick their download times are (the time it takes for the Web site to appear on your customers' browsers) and how effective their e-mail services are. If visitors to your Web site are frustrated with the service of your ISP it reflects on your business.

Further information on the different ISPs available can be found at dir.yahoo.com/Business_and_Economy/Communications_and _Networking/Internet_and_World_Wide_Web/Network_Service_ Providers/Internet_Service_Providers_ISPs/.

Summary

Although the Internet is a fast-paced medium, the secret to successful e-marketing is careful and well thought out preparation. This involves working out not only what equipment you will need and how much money you can spend, but also how to match your objectives with those of your audience. It also involves substantial Internet research. The tools and techniques involved in researching your online market are discussed in the next chapter.

two

E-market
research

Research is the foundation upon which all online marketing activity should be built. If you fail to conduct comprehensive research, it will be almost impossible to target your audience effectively. As the Internet is, first and foremost, an information resource, it is in many ways the perfect market research tool. It enables you to search for business information around the world, get an insight into the activities of your competitors and gauge the opinions of your target customers. Furthermore, owing to search engine technology, relevant information can be searched for very quickly. The aim of this chapter is to look at the benefits of the Internet as a research tool, focusing on how it can be used to gather the sort of information that will add value to your e-marketing efforts.

Market research and the Internet

E-market research refers to research into your online market conducted via the Internet. As an online marketer the reasons for conducting Internet research are twofold. First, it is important to study the online market in order to analyse trends and fluctuations that may affect your own online business activity. Secondly, as a medium characterized by information and interaction, the Internet is the most effective tool both for discovering data compiled by other people and for coming up with new findings yourself.

The type of primary and secondary data you look for, of course, will relate to the specific focus of your business and (if you already have one) your Web site. However, the information you uncover can also help you find and develop that focus in the first place. By researching the activity of your competition, the habits of your potential customers and the general state of your industry or sector as a whole, you will be able to direct your e-marketing strategy with confidence. For instance, online research can give you the information needed to differentiate your Web site from its competitors.

Perhaps the most important criterion for conducting research on the Internet is to keep an open mind. As Matt Perry from Internet Marketing firm Net Marketeers puts it, 'There is little point in using information as a way of validating conclusions you have already come up with before embarking online.' As with all your online activities, you should adopt a flexible and opportunistic approach and be prepared to change direction if and when necessary.

Due to the sheer size and multifunctional nature of the Internet, the most daunting part of e-market research is knowing where to start. Generally speaking, the major search engines should be your first port of call as they will help you find and prioritize background information on your online market.

Using search engines

To find the information you need on the Internet, you will need to use search engines. Without the aid of search engines, navigating your way around the millions of Web pages would be a near impossible task. The technology search engines use to search through vast indexes of Web sites makes your job a lot easier as it prioritizes information based on the keywords you type in. However, even *with* the help of search engines market research can be an uphill struggle if you don't know how to get the most out of them. Here are some general guidelines to follow for effective searching:

- *Be specific.* Never rely on just one generic keyword to conduct a search. As Brian Pinkerton from Web Crawler says, 'Imagine walking up to a librarian and saying "travel". They're going to look at you with a blank face.' Use qualifying words to make searches more specific.
- *Visit various search engines.* As each search engine indexes and prioritizes information according to different criteria, it is always a good idea to use several of them. Otherwise you could be missing out on information which, although you consider it relevant, one of the search engines has failed to pick up.

■ *Conduct 'plain English' searches.* One of the easiest ways to use search engines involves carrying out a 'plain English' search. This means that instead of relying on keywords you can type in a natural language question such as, 'Where can I find information on Web site design firms in London?' Ask Jeeves (www.askjeeeves.com – co.uk) is probably the most famous 'plain English' search engine, although Alta Vista (www.altavista.com) enables you to conduct natural language searches alongside regular keyword searches.

The main search sites

There are literally thousands of search engines on the Web covering general areas as well as more specific topics. Each search engine indexes and organizes information in completely different ways. For instance, some search engines rely solely on 'robots' to categorize information based on keywords embedded in a Web site's HTML code (the Web building code), while others prefer to depend on human judgement. Outlined below is a brief rundown of the search sites that are most likely to assist your market research efforts.

AltaVista (www.altavista.com – co.uk)
Alta Vista is one of the longest running search engines on the Web and remains among the most popular. As we will see, Alta Vista enables you to narrow searches using specific commands and also allows you to conduct 'plain English' searches. In addition to its search box, the Alta Vista home page enables you to link to 'Current News Stories' and 'Frequently Used Links' sections.

Ask Jeeves (www.askjeeves.com – co.uk)
As well as enabling you to conduct searches in plain English, Ask Jeeves also breaks down its directory into various sections. These sections include 'Money', 'Travel', 'Health', 'Shopping' and 'Computers'.

Excite (www.excite.com – co.uk)
Excite is another popular site, partly due to its Power Search option. The Power Search enables you to customize your search matchings to a greater extent than a standard keywords search allows. Another reason why Excite is popular among e-marketers

is its NewsTracker service. NewsTracker tracks the news from hundreds of online publications and searches for specified keywords.

HotBot (www.hotbot.com)
HotBot provides a 'SuperSearch' option that again enables you to fine tune your search according to specific criteria.

Infoseek (www.infoseek.com)
As well as the search box, the Infoseek home page contains links to categories and sub-categories that you can access to find specific information about one topic.

Lycos (www.lycos.com – co.uk)
Lycos combines sophisticated technology with a more human approach in its Top 5 per cent Web sites link, where site reviewers pick their top sites within different categories. If you want to refine your search, click on the 'Search Options' link and fill in the detailed search form before clicking on the 'Go Get It' button.

Northern Light (www.northernlight.com)
Alongside its main Web index, Northern Light includes a 'Special Collection' consisting of news articles and content from press wires (news services such as Reuters). The other unique aspect of Northern Light is that it groups its search findings into Custom Search Folders. Once you have conducted a search, you can open the folder that fits most closely with the type of information you want.

Yahoo! (www.yahoo.com – co.uk)
Although Yahoo! is generally referred to as a search engine it is in fact a directory with a search engine (Google) attached. As a directory, humans as opposed to search engine robots index sites and information is organized into categories such as 'computers', 'business and finance' and 'media' (see Figure 2.1). By clicking on the 'Options' button on the home page you will be provided with a form that will help you to limit your search. Yahoo! also enables you to conduct either international or domestic searches. Furthermore, Yahoo's People Search section (which can be addressed via the main home page) allows you to search for e-mail addresses and other contact details.

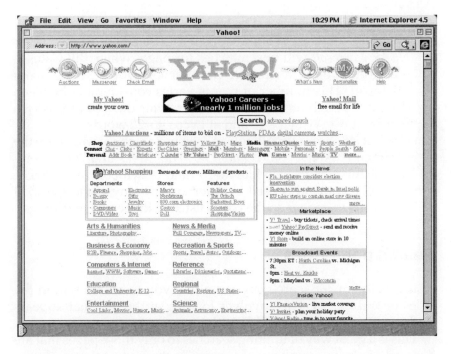

Figure 2.1 Yahoo! Web site. Yahoo! enables you to limit your searches in various ways

Using search commands

As well as making sure your keyword phrases and commands are as specific as possible, on many of the search engines you can use special search commands to narrow searches further. Here are some of the most widely accepted techniques to add more focus to your searches:

- *Use + and – symbols.* The + (plus) and – (minus) symbols can be used to provide search engines with a better idea of the sort of information you are looking for. For example if you typed in the command *Gates + Microsoft* the search engine would display all the pages on its index that mention both Bill Gates and Microsoft. If you then entered the Command *Gates + Microsoft – Internet* it would cut pages down to only those that don't mention the Internet.
- *Place keywords in quotation marks.* By placing a string of keywords within quotation marks you can limit your search to only those pages where the words appear in exactly the order you specify.

- *Use the NEAR command.* The NEAR command is used to specify how close keywords should appear together. For instance, *Gates NEAR Microsoft* will find matches for pages where Bill Gates is mentioned only a certain number of words away from Microsoft. This number of words varies considerably between different search engines. At Web Crawler the distance is two words, at AltaVista it's 10 and at Lycos it's 25 words.
- *Conduct a Boolean search.* Boolean searches are those which use the commands 'AND', 'NOT' and 'OR'. The 'AND' and 'NOT' commands function exactly like the '+' and '-' symbols respectively. The OR command is used in order to allow any of the specified keywords to appear on the pages listed in the search matchings.

Search page titles

Many of the major search engines allow you to search within the titles of Web pages. This involves looking at the text that appears within the title tag of an HTML Web document.

This is a great way of limiting searches to only those pages that are focused solely on your keyword topic. To conduct a title search you need to place the command 'title:' before keywords in a search box. (The title: command doesn't work at Lycos or Yahoo. At Lycos, you need to use the advanced search page to do a title search. At Yahoo, you must instead use the t: command to search through titles.) Several of the search engines that support the title command also allow you to specify a title search using their advanced search pages.

If you want to narrow a search even further, you can visit the AltaVista search engine (www.altavista.com), where you can use these additional commands:

- *url:* Placing the *url:* command before a keyword will limit the searches to Web site addresses (technically referred to as URLs or Uniform Resource Locators). Lycos also enables you to conduct a URL search via its advanced search form.
- *Domain:* The *domain:* command offers the ability to limit searches to domain suffixes such as .com or .co.uk. Therefore if you entered *chocolate+domain:.co.uk* your search would be limited to chocolate Web sites based in the UK.
- *Text:* Placing '*Text:*' at the beginning of your keyword entry will help you limit a search to actual text, as opposed to image titles and links.

Help pages

Many search engines provide more information on how to narrow searches within their help pages. Here are some of the most useful addresses:

AltaVista Help (doc.altavista.com/help/search/search_help)
Excite Search Help (www.excite.com/Info)
Google Help (www.google.com/intl/en_extra/help/index.html)
GoTo Search Tips (www.goto.com/d/about/help)
HotBot Search Tips (www.hotbot.com/help/tips)
Infoseek How To Search (www.infoseek.com)
Lycos Help (www.lycos.com/help/)
Northern Light Search Help
    (www.northernlight.com/docs/search_help_optimize.html)
WebCrawler Help (www.webcrawler.com/Info/)
Yahoo Advanced Search Options (search.yahoo.com/search/options)

Conducting a meta-search

As conducting individual searches on each major search engine takes a considerable amount of time, you may find it more convenient to visit meta-search sites. These are search engines that search the main engines simultaneously. Of course, if you do decide to use a meta-search site as part of your market research activity you must try to make each search as specific as possible. Use the operators + and – to narrow your search further, or you will end up with a severe case of 'information overload'. Here is an overview of the main meta-search engines.

Mamma (www.mamma.com)
The Mamma search engine (see Figure 2.2) searches Alta Vista, Excite, HotBot, Infoseek, Lycos, Webcrawler and Yahoo! to find relevant information. Mamma provides a brief summary of each page in your results and enables you to restrict searches to page titles only.

MetaCrawler (www.metacrawler.com)
MetaCrawler was among the first meta-search sites to appear and is still extremely popular. Due to the vast number of Web pages it

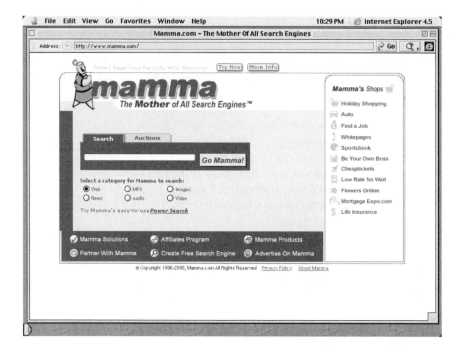

Figure 2.2 Mamma Web site. The Mamma search engine enables you to search all the major search sites at one time

trawls through, it enables you to limit searches to different Web site categories such as news, finance and entertainment. To find information MetaCrawler searches the databases of AltaVista, Excite, Infoseek, Lycos, Thunderstone and Yahoo! In addition, the site offers a Deja-like service, enabling you to search through thousands of Usenet discussion groups. For a highly specialized search MetaCrawler provides a 'Power Search' option, which involves filling in a form and submitting more detailed instructions relating to the information you require.

Savvy Search (www.savvysearch.com)

The Savvy Search site enables you to conduct searches under different categories, such as news, newspapers and magazine articles. In addition it conducts one of the broadest meta-searches available, searching through Alta Vista, Direct Hit, Excite, Galaxy, Google, HotBot, Infoseek, National Directory, Thunderstone and Web Crawler.

Create your own directory

As research is an ongoing process, you may find it useful to create your own directory of relevant sites using the 'Bookmark' facility provided by the two main Web browsers, Internet Explorer and Netscape Navigator. The great thing about bookmarks is that they enable you to categorize sites into various folders and sub-folders. Therefore, no matter how many sites you decide to bookmark you will be able to find them easily.

If you want to take this DIY approach to the next level you could even invest in some search software. This can enable you to search the Web for keywords and phrases even when you are not connected to the Internet. Once you have entered the relevant words into the program, the search process is automatic. These programs keep you informed of any new additions to the Web which contain your keywords, and can therefore help you monitor the Web for mentions of your own company or domain name. Some of the most popular search software products are available at Intelliseek (www.intelliseek.com), Copernic (www.copernic.com) and Inforian (www.inforian.com).

Primary research

So far this chapter has mainly focused on the ways the Internet can be used to find information that has already been compiled for someone else for some other purpose. This is what market researchers refer to as 'secondary research'. While this type of research is essential for any market research campaign it needs to be supplemented with new findings you have collected yourself, in other words primary research. After all, research you have conducted yourself will be more likely to be relevant to your own specific online marketing activity. It will be more up to date and more directly applicable to your Web site than information collected previously for a different reason.

Market research practitioners divide primary research into two categories: quantitative and qualitative. Quantitative research is used to find fixed answers to closed questions such as, 'How much would you be willing to pay for this product?' Any information that can be expressed using a numerical measure is considered quantitative. Typically, quantitative research involves sending out surveys with multiple choice answers. This helps marketers break down information into percentages and set figures.

Qualitative research is concerned with information that is based on thoughts and feelings as opposed to quantifiable, hard facts. Accordingly, qualitative research involves asking open questions such as, 'Why do you prefer product x to product y?' or, 'What do you feel about our new range of services?'

The Internet is a highly effective medium for both types of primary research. As it enables you to reach thousands of people for little or no expense, it provides a very convenient way of sending out quantitative surveys. Furthermore, as the Internet has been shown to encourage more honest opinions than face-to-face interviews and focus groups, it can add to the validity of qualitative research.

E-mail as a research tool

While the World Wide Web provides researchers with a mine of secondary data, e-mail is the perfect medium for primary research. Although many people view the Web as synonymous with the Internet, e-mail is in fact a far more widely used Internet application. Furthermore, when most people use the Web they do not directly participate in it. E-mail, on the other hand, is designed for communication and therefore involves the end user at a much deeper level. Whereas most people who use the Web don't have their own Web addresses, everyone who uses e-mail has to have their own e-mail account. This goes to show that e-mail provides a degree of access to people that isn't afforded by the Web. In addition, e-mail also provides the following benefits:

- *Cost.* Surveys can be sent out to thousands of Internet users at minimal expense.
- *Speed.* As people generally respond to their e-mails within 24 hours, e-mail provides researchers with almost instant results.
- *Reach.* E-mail enables you to conduct research among target audiences around the globe as long distances and different time zones no longer pose a problem.
- *Response rates.* E-mail questionnaires and surveys can receive a better response as they reach respondents when users are more likely to answer because, generally speaking, people opening their e-mail are prepared to interact.

E-mail not only makes a response more likely, but it can also increase the validity of that response. Adam Joinson, a psychologist at the Open University, certainly found this to be the case when he conducted a study looking into levels of self-disclosure in e-mail and other forms of communication. It emerged that compared to face-to-face conversation, e-mail is four times as likely to provoke an honest response. In an interview with *The Guardian* newspaper, Joinson concluded that, 'When they can't see each other, people are more focused and less concerned about being judged. When using e-mail we can concentrate on the message, not the way we represent it.' This view is supported by Kevin Roberts, chief executive for the US division of Saatchi and Saatchi. He told me: 'The biggest revelation around the Internet is not e-commerce, it's e-motion. People open up and share how they feel on the net, something they just don't do in more classical research formats such as focus groups. They open up and start a dialogue, a relationship, a connection.'

Of course, to conduct research via e-mail you will need a list of relevant e-mail addresses to send to. (We will explore in more detail the ways in which you can compile an e-mailing list further on in this book.) Once you have a mailing list of 'opt in' subscribers (people who are willing to receive e-mail messages from you), a survey questionnaire could either be incorporated within a newsletter or sent out as a separate mailing. Here is some advice on putting together an e-mail questionnaire:

- *Keep it brief.* The longer the questionnaire is, the less likely it is that it will be completed.
- *Provide an explanation.* Explain the purpose of the questionnaire and why the recipient's answers will be important.
- *Use a Web design package.* You can create questionnaires using a Web building tool such as Dreamweaver or Microsoft Front Page. This enables you to make it more visually attractive by adding colour and graphics. This will increase the recipient's willingness to spend more time answering the questionnaire.
- *Include a link to your site.* Placing a link back to your site will help increase repeat traffic.
- *Offer an incentive.* In order to make sure at least some of the recipients complete and return the questionnaire, offer a gift or entry into a competition to the people who make the effort.
- *Use the Bcc: function.* When you send the same questionnaire out to lots of people simultaneously, place all the e-mail addresses

in the Bcc: (Blind Carbon Copy) box. This will ensure that all the addresses remain invisible to each recipient.

- *Personalize.* Where possible, you should send a personalized message with each questionnaire. While this may be unrealistic when you are conducting a large-scale quantitative research campaign, it is worth making the effort when you are sending out questionnaires to a small sample group.
- *Provide advance notice.* Sending out a brief e-mail message in advance of the questionnaire can help to encourage a good response. You could even send out a notice asking if people will be willing to fill in the questionnaire. This will prevent you irritating people who wouldn't want to complete it. It is also worth bearing in mind that advance notices that go out closer to the questionnaire mailing time produce better results than those sent out too far in advance.
- *Compile stimulating questions.* If you make questions imaginative or humorous, recipients will be less reluctant to fill in the form. Wine Cellar (www.winecellar.co.uk) is one online company that adopts a humorous approach in its multiple-choice questionnaires.

Newsgroup research

The Internet is about much more than just Web sites and e-mail. Indeed, one of the most fertile areas for online market research is the collection of news and discussion groups referred to as Usenet. There are over 100,000 discussion groups, which focus on every topic imaginable. These groups are divided into different categories, each category consisting of around 10,000 groups. The main categories are as follows (they are listed with their official Usenet description):

- *alt (alternative).* Anything goes type discussions covering every conceivable topic from aliens to Zen.
- *biz (business).* Discussion about business products and services, including product debuts, upgrades, enhancements and reviews.
- *comp (computers).* Discussions about hardware, software, languages, systems. Also, valuable consumer advice.
- *humanities.* Literature, fine arts and other humanities, for both professionals and amateurs.

- *news*. Information regarding the Usenet news network and software, including news servers and news headers.
- *rec (recreation)*. Discussions about arts, games, hobbies, music, sports, etc.
- *soc (society)*. Discussions of social issues and culture, as well as a place to socialize.

All the groups within the above categories are indexed and archived on the Deja News Web site (www.deja.com). The Deja site enables you to search all the Usenet groups simultaneously. As its homepage declares, Deja can help you 'harness the knowledge of millions of people to answer questions, research purchases or debate issues'. While these groups often greet blatantly commercial messages with disdain, it is perfectly acceptable to ask people questions that may help your business. For instance, if you plan to sell coffee online you could legitimately post the following message to a coffee-lovers discussion group: 'Hi, I'm in the process of shifting my coffee business online. Who would you consider to be my main competitors?'

It is possible, however, to conduct discussion group research without contributing to the group. In fact, an estimated three out of four people who read discussion groups do not participate. If your Web site is already up and running you can search the newsgroups for mentions of your company.

Competitor research

The easiest way to find out about your competitors is to visit their Web sites. If you are unsure as to who exactly your competitors are, you will need to visit the major search engines and type in the sort of keywords or phrases that someone would use to find a site like yours. The search findings will show you not only sites offering similar products or services, but also the competitors your customers are likely to visit. Don't just limit your search to the top 10 search results, because many of your direct competitors may be ranked a lot lower than that.

Make sure you keep an open mind as you search rival sites. After all, they could end up being associated partners. When you visit competitor sites look out for information that could influence your own online marketing strategy. This could include:

- *Advertising.* Check to see if anyone advertises on your competitors' sites. If they do, it could be worth posing as a potential advertiser to find out how much their advertising rates are. This will also enable you to discover other relevant information (such as the number of visitors they have, where their target market is based, what age range they cater for and so on).
- *Forums.* If the site includes some sort of online forum (such as a bulletin board or chat room) you may be able to find out what visitors are saying about the company. It will also give you an idea of how successful these interactive features can be.
- *E-commerce.* Do your competitors sell products and services online, or are their sites used to add brand support to their offline activity? If they do sell products online, look to see if a lot of effort is required on the part of the site visitor to make a purchase. Ask yourself, 'How could this process be simplified?' Look also to see if the site is a member of any e-trader schemes, and if they are find out which ones. This might help you work out who you should contact in order to receive similar seals of approval from e-commerce organizations.
- *Mailing lists.* If a site has a mailing list, subscribe to it. This will enable you to receive even more relevant information. If they offer an online newsletter it may also provide you with useful material on your industry or market as a whole, and could provide you with some pointers regarding the content of your newsletter.
- *Design.* As well as looking at the visual features and graphic elements of a site's design, you should also look out for how the Web site design functions. In other words, analyse the way the site is put together. Is it cohesive? Is it easy to navigate, or do you end up getting lost? Look carefully at what you think works well and not so well.
- *HTML.* As you may know, HTML is the computer code used to display information on the Web. Incorporated within a site's HTML are 'meta-tags'. These are instructions that are used to inform search engines of a Web site's content. By looking at the meta-tags used by your competitors, you will be able to work out the keywords and descriptions they give to search engines in order to get their high ranking. To view the HTML text behind Web pages you will need to click on the 'View' option on your Web browser and then go into 'Source'.

The HTML text will then automatically appear on your computer screen.

 - *Updates.* Another thing to look out for on competitor sites is the last time the site was updated. Some sites will be updated almost continuously while others will be left untouched.

As well as looking out for what *is* included on a competitor's Web site you should also be looking out for what is missing. If you find something that isn't included on other sites that you think should be, you can then add it to your own site to create a point of difference. As we will see later on in this book, differentiation is the key to building a strong and successful e-brand. After all, by promoting an area of your site that you know is unique, you will be providing Internet users with a real and positive reason to visit your site rather than your competitors'.

As well as using search engines to try to find out what your competitors are up to on the Web you should also visit any relevant trade organization Web sites. These often provide a directory of links to the sites of their members. Also, if you are researching public limited companies, visit Daily Stocks (www.dailystocks.com) which links to a variety of sites providing information on international companies.

Market research via your site

Once your Web site is up and running, it can be used in various ways to conduct primary research. As we shall see in the concluding chapter, incorporating online forums such as discussion groups and chat rooms within Web sites can provide marketers with useful feedback relating to their marketing efforts. E-mail links can also be used to collect feedback and comments from site visitors. Carrying out market research at your site is important because it can provide insight into why people have chosen to visit you rather than your competition. However, if you are asking people to help you in your research efforts you will probably need to offer some form of incentive. For instance, when the online confectioner Jelly Belly (www.jellybelly.com) invited customers to fill in an online questionnaire, free jellybeans were offered as a reward for completing the form.

Most Web design software packages enable you to create a form by providing you with the essential elements (text boxes, radio buttons, check boxes, drop-down menus, submit buttons) to transfer straight to your site. If you are creating a form page using raw HTML it is a bit more complicated, but plenty of advice can be found at The Barebones Guide to HTML (www.werbach.com/barebones). If you want to conduct qualitative research and ask open questions you will need to use *text boxes*. These are blank boxes into which visitors type free-form responses to the given question. If, however, you are conducting qualitative research and are asking closed questions you will be better off using *drop-down boxes* where visitors make a selection from a drop-down list.

Generally speaking, surveys using drop-down boxes tend to receive a better response as they involve less effort on the part of the visitor. They can fill in the whole form in a matter of minutes.

Automated research

The radical effect the Internet has had on market research in general is evidenced by Insight Express (www.insightexpress.com), the world's first, though undoubtedly not the last, automated online market research service. Insight Express enables companies to put together a survey in a matter of minutes (by adapting one of its templates), send it to a sample group relevant to their business and get hundreds of responses within a matter of hours. Although the service was initiated in the US it looks set to expand internationally and certain to spawn European imitators.

Practically anything you want to gauge opinion on, such as your catch line, mission statement or Web design can be put to the online focus groups. When a company has put a survey together, Insight Express sends out its banner advertisements to sites with a suitable audience profile (for instance, if you sell baby products the banners would appear on parent and baby sites) and asks people to respond. The service can also send out market research surveys to a broader cross-section of the online community via international advertising agency networks such as 24/7 Media (www.247media.com) and Double Click (www.doubleclick.com).

Market researchers are already finding that this type of service provides two distinct advantages over offline methods: cost and speed. Surveys average at around $1000 (£600) which, although it may be out of reach for a small business, is much lower than the cost of getting a market research firm to conduct focus group opinion testing on a similar scale offline. The speed factor is even more significant. In the real world it can take months to target suitable population segments, bring focus groups together and then evaluate the findings. On the Internet the whole process can be carried out within 24 hours.

To see how it works in practice, Paul Hochman, a US-based journalist, tried out the service for *eCompany* magazine: 'I put together a quick survey on who among Oprah Winfrey, Michael Jordan, Bart Simpson, Tiger Woods and Bill Clinton might be the best spokesperson for a new brand of toothpaste. Not surprisingly, Oprah was most popular (22.8 per cent), but Bart Simpson grabbed second with 11.29 per cent, beating Tiger Woods, Bill Clinton and Michael Jordan.' However, as Hochman discovered, these findings 'may be suspect' as 'more than 2 per cent of respondents said they never brush their teeth'.

Getting information to come to you

One way to save time while conducting research is to get information to come to you. There are various ways in which you can be provided with relevant information on a regular basis without having to return to a Web site. Here are some of them:

- *Join mailing lists.* By subscribing to relevant mailing lists you will receive a regular flow of useful information via your e-mail box. A comprehensive index of mailing lists can be found at NeoSoft (www.neosoft.com).
- *Subscribe to push channels.* Push channels are Internet-based services that send out their content via e-mail. Pointcast (www.pointcast.com) is one such service, providing a wide range of general interest and business information.
- *Use personalized news providers.* News services such as Infobeat (www.infobeat.com) and the UK-based Ananova (www.ananova.com) enable you to create your own customized newspaper that can then be sent to your e-mail address. Once you specify the information you are interested in, and prioritize that information, the service will provide you with updates as and when relevant stories emerge.

Useful research sites

The following sites are all useful sources of secondary research:

- *Audit Bureau of Circulation (www.abc.org.uk).* The Audit Bureau of Circulation site is particularly useful when you are researching a media campaign as it provides circulation figures and other relevant information for around 4000 UK publications, both online and offline.
- *Cyber Atlas (www.cyberatlas.internet.com).* Internet.com's Cyber Atlas service provides facts and figures relating to international Web trends.
- *Media Metrix (www.mediametrix.com).* Media Metrix provides charts of the most popular Web sites and various other e-media statistics.
- *eMarketer (www.emarketer.com).* As well as providing statistics on Internet usage, the eMarketer site also provides detailed reports. These reports, as the eMarketer homepage makes clear, provide 'aggregated data, key stats, original analysis on online advertising and marketing, user demographics and trends, and the world-wide e-commerce market place'.
- *Search Engine Watch (www.searchenginewatch.com).* Search Engine Watch is full of useful advice on how to get the most out of search engines. It also provides search engine news, reviews and comparative analysis.
- *European Business News (www.eubusiness.com).* This site provides comprehensive and up-to-date market news with a European slant.
- *ClickZ (www.clickz.com).* ClickZ is an online marketing magazine providing regular features on market research methods from marketing consultants and journalists.
- *Marketing Tips (www.marketingtips.com).* The Marketing Tips site provides tips on practically every aspect of marketing, including market research.
- *Beaucoup (www.beaucoup.com).* Beacucoup is a directory of over 1000 specialist search engines.

Summary

As the epitome of the Information Age, it is little surprise that the Internet can be a useful research tool. Enabling you to conduct both primary and secondary research, it can help you gain a comprehensive picture of your online market. It is important to remember, however, that e-market research isn't just something that precedes marketing activity, but is in fact an ongoing process. Owing to the frenetic pace of the Internet market, trends and situations change all the time. It is only by constantly keeping track of your online market that you will be able to anticipate external factors that may affect your business, in both the short and long term.

three

The Web design **dilemma**

Once you have researched your online market, you will then be able to start thinking about developing your Web site. This is the point at which some serious decision making needs to happen. The dilemma companies face is whether to design a Web site in-house or use an external agency. To make this decision, you will need to draw on your own online market research and reassess your e-marketing objectives. Specifically, you will also need to put together a plan for your Web site. Even if you decide to use a Web design agency, this plan will help to keep your Web site objectives on track. Therefore, before we discuss the pros and cons inherent in each side of the design dilemma, it will be useful to look at how you should start planning your Web site strategy.

Design planning

Thorough planning is an integral part of the Web design process. Before you rush headlong into a dizzying maze of HTML code or the even more disorientating realm of the Web design agency, you need to think very carefully about what your Web site objectives are and how these objectives will be reached.

Before you do anything else you should assess your Web design goals by asking yourself the following questions.

Which audiences are you targeting?

Defining your target audiences helps you to develop the content and character of your Web site. As a business you are likely to have a multitude of audiences. These may include existing customers, potential customers, consumers, business clients, investors, suppliers, industry pundits, competitors, advertisers and sponsors. Even within each audience category it may be possible to make distinctions, for instance between a domestic and international market. The main aim of your site might be to attract a consumer audience, but you might also want to cater for businesses (eg, advertisers) as well. This means you will have to create a separate sub-section within your site that caters for this secondary audience.

Contrary to what you may think, having more than one audience does not mean you will have to dilute your site's brand identity. What it does mean, however, is that you will have to prioritize which audience is the most important. For instance WorldPop.com (www.worldpop.com), the successful pop music site, caters for both a consumer and business audience, but realizes its focus must be geared heavily towards the consumer. It satisfies its business audience by providing a link on the home page that instructs users to click 'for advertising and other commercial opportunities'. This leads to a separate B2B (business-to-business) section that gives a full list of useful e-mail and phone contacts for WorldPop's various business audiences.

If your online audiences are really diverse you may even need to consider the possibility of having more than one Web site. If, for instance, you have a wide array of products that appeal to diverse groups of consumers, you could take the Procter and Gamble approach and build a Web site for every one of your products. If your audiences are geographically and culturally diverse you could set up different Web sites for each country/language. Whenever possible, you should try and test your site on members of your target audience(s) as you build it. This will provide you with useful feedback that will enable you to rearrange and refine your site if necessary, so you can tailor the site to fit the audience.

Why do you want a Web site?

As virtually any business worth its salt now has an online presence, this question may initially seem something of a no-brainer. It is important, however, to assess *exactly* what marketing goals you want your site to achieve. Here are some examples of common Web site objectives:

- to generate new sales leads/increase sales;
- to establish a leading presence within your online business community;
- to increase customer loyalty;
- to consolidate your brand identity;
- to expand into overseas markets;
- to offer 24-hour customer support;
- to create an online community relevant to your audience;
- to attract job-hunters;
- to increase the customer's 'lifetime value'.

When you are formulating objectives you need to remember that they are not set in stone. For instance, your initial objective may only be 'to increase sales'. Over time, however, this may evolve into other, more specific, aims such as 'to create an online community' or 'to attract advertisers'. Thinking about what you want your site to achieve, and even writing down these objectives on paper, will provide you with the focus needed to design a coherent site. Each time you come across a difficult design decision, you will be able to refer back to these objectives to help you decide how best to move forward.

What do you want to happen when people are at your site?

Related to the question of why you want a Web site is the issue of what you actually want Internet users to do once they have made their way to your site. To help you decide what you want to happen, you should bear in mind the four main reasons why people log onto the Internet:

1. to find information;
2. to interact with other Internet users;
3. to be entertained;
4. to shop.

If your site fails to satisfy any of the above criteria then nothing will happen at your site. Furthermore, thinking from the perspective of what your target audience(s) want to get out of the Internet will help you tailor the site to meet their interests. For instance, once you have decided that the main aim of your site is to provide people with useful information this decision will influence the layout of your site. The emphasis will be on creating a straightforward and user-friendly design, rather than on diverting people with an array of flashing gizmos and novelty links.

Likewise, if one of your aims is for people to interact with each other this will influence the structure of your site. Chat rooms, bulletin boards and other interactive elements would all have to be considered when planning the site's layout.

How much are you prepared to spend?

Before you start designing your Web site, you need to work out exactly how much time and money you can afford to invest. Once you have attached a monetary figure to your site, you will then be able to work out its precise scale and scope. Your budget will help you not only to determine your objectives, but also how you are going to build your site. Web design firms can be very expensive, and are therefore not a valid option for every business. Then again, the time and effort they save you may make outsourcing worthwhile. Professional looking Web sites *can* come cheap, but they do depend on a lot of hard work and creative energy.

Mapping out your site

Whether you are hiring an external agency to build your site or are designing it completely yourself, it is advisable to map out your vision of how it should be structured beforehand. Putting together a plan or flowchart which details how the Web pages will link with each other will force you to think carefully about each individual section as well as providing a 'bird's eye view' of the site as a whole.

You can start by putting together a straightforward flowchart of all the pages in the site. This is what Web designers and other multimedia types refer to as a 'site architecture' or 'site blueprint'. Once you have done this, you can then home in on the design elements of each individual page. This will help you figure out the balance of text, animated graphics and audio-visual files throughout your site. Once you can see in your mind's eye how each page should look, you could then use a graphic design program such as Adobe Page Maker or Quark Express to lay out the pages on a computer screen.

This will enable you to play about with different visual ideas to see what works and what doesn't.

The Web design options

When you have decided what you want your Web site to achieve, your next step is to work out *how* you are going to build your site. You can either hire someone else to build it for you, or build it yourself using Web design software or working with raw HTML code. Outlined below is an overview of each option.

Hiring a Web design agency

The Web design industry is growing at an increasingly rapid rate, as more and more offline companies are placing ever more emphasis on the Internet. The *advantages* of using a Web design agency include:

- *Expertise*. Web design firms offer clients expertise of both computer programming and graphic design.
- *Time*. Outsourcing your Web requirements is going to save you a lot of time and effort (in theory at least).
- *Ongoing support*. Increasingly, Web design firms are able to offer their clients ongoing design and marketing support.
- *Advice*. Web designers can provide you with an informed opinion as to what will work and what won't.
- *Technology*. Web design firms have access to a broad range of state-of-the-art hardware and software and, more significantly, know what to do with it.

The *disadvantages* of using a Web design agency include:

- *Cost*. It goes without saying that if you are going to hire someone else to design your site it is going to be more expensive than if you did it yourself.
- *Limited knowledge*. While design agencies may know a lot about Web sites they only have a limited knowledge of your company.
- *Imbalanced outlook*. Web design firms can place too much emphasis on programming at the expense of graphic design (and vice versa).

- *Risk.* When you hand over Web design responsibilities you are losing an element of control over the process, and therefore increasing risk.
- *Content.* Web designers and copywriters are unlikely to know as much about your industry as you do, and therefore may not be the best source of Web site content.

The best way to choose a Web design agency is via personal recommendation. Failing that, you should look for sites you think are successful and find out who designed them. The Internet Works Web site (www.iwks.com) provides a comprehensive list of Web design firms and freelance design consultants incorporating also a cross-section of their clients.

When you have found a company that seems to match your budget and design objectives, interrogate them with the following questions:

- Can I see your client list?
- Do you focus on specific sectors (eg, B2B) or do you cater for anyone?
- Do you have standard charges or do rates vary?
- Do you offer a copywriting service?
- What will you need from our company?
- Does this project excite you? Why?
- Will you be able to provide ongoing support if required?
- Do you deal with meta-tags? (Meta-tags are commands that help search engines rank your site.)
- What other e-marketing services do you provide?
- How experienced are your staff?
- Who will be working on our company site?

If you are unsure about your first choice, shop around. There are hundreds of Web design firms out there, each providing different types of services for different types of clients.

Using Web design software

Web building software provides you with a relatively simple and straightforward means of creating your own Web pages. Instead of having to deal directly with the Web building HTML commands yourself, these software products convert the HTML for you.

Indeed if you can use a word processing program, you will have little problem in using a 'WYSIWYG' package. (WYSIWYG stands for 'What You See Is What You Get' and it is a suitable acronym attached to software packages that promise that what you design on your screen will look exactly the same when transferred to the Web.) If you know how to point and click your mouse and type on a keyboard, these packages won't give you too much of a headache. Many packages now include *design templates*, which make Web design even easier by providing 'off-the-peg' design features such as forms, buttons, banners and other graphic icons.

Here's a brief overview of three of the most popular Web design packages:

- *Microsoft Front Page*. Microsoft's Web design software is probably the most widely used in the world. It takes you through the Web building process step-by-step, and provides lots of extensions for when you are feeling more adventurous. It also comes in a free version (without extensions) called Microsoft Front Page Express.
- *Dreamweaver*. Macromedia's Dreamweaver tends to be the graphic designer's choice, providing you with all the tools you need to build a good-looking and user-friendly site.
- *Adobe GoLive*. Adobe GoLive is quite an advanced WYSIWYG package, providing an equal emphasis on the form and function of Web design.

All of the above packages are continuously updated with new versions appearing on the market approximately once a year. Although none of these packages are particularly expensive, it is worth looking out for the free versions that often come as part of a CD package on the front cover of Internet magazines.

All three packages provide detailed instructions on how they should be used and each provides enough features for you to be able to tailor your site for its own specific purposes. If, however, you are intending your site to offer e-commerce procedures you may need to supplement Web building software with special 'shopping cart' or 'shop in a box' software products. This is because HTML, although perfectly efficient at creating order forms, cannot actually make forms *do* anything. For your business to be able to handle credit card transactions and any other payment processes online, you will need to invest in special software that will enable your site not only to incorporate order forms but also to be able to interpret and calculate the information that a user enters. As well as being able to conduct calculations these shop in a box packages can also provide payment recording, customer account tracking and inventory control. You can buy a shop 'off the shelf' using very straightforward shop building products such as Click and Build (www.clickandbuild.com), which enables you to cut and paste a workable order form directly onto your site. It can also help you to build an e-commerce site from scratch, although packages such as these don't offer a great deal of sophistication in terms of Web design elements. More advanced, and often more expensive, shop building alternatives can be found at the following sites: Open Market (www.openmarket.com), Intershop (www.intershop.com) and Maestro Commerce (www.maestrocommerce.com).

Using HTML

HTML (Hyper Text Mark-up Language) is the code, or rather 'language', which converts data (text, graphics and so on) into Web pages. Although it remains invisible to Web site visitors, without it their Web browser would not be able to display the information contained on your Web page. In fact, it is impossible to build a Web site without using HTML. That is not to say you will have to learn this coding language yourself however. You can use a Web building software package (such as those mentioned above) which shields you from the gritty HTML details, or you can hire a Web design firm that will work with the raw HTML on your behalf. Having said this, working directly with HTML does offer the e-marketer some obvious advantages, including:

- *Net knowledge.* Using HTML will increase your understanding of how the Web is put together, and will therefore enable you to manipulate 'the architecture of the Web' in your favour.
- *Cost.* Working directly with HTML commands is obviously the cheapest Web building option.
- *Ongoing value.* Once you have built your site with HTML, you will be able to make amendments as and when you choose. Therefore, you will not need to revisit a Web design agency or buy the latest software upgrades.
- *Search engines.* Meta-tags (which are a type of HTML command) are used by search engines to interpret your site content. They are therefore vital if you are to ensure a good search engine ranking. Many Web design firms and most software packages ignore meta-tags altogether.

■ *Personalization.* A sound knowledge of the main HTML commands will enable you to tailor your site exactly the way you want it. You won't have to resort to cutting and pasting 'one size fits all' Web features, as you might if you depend solely on Web building software.

■ *Added value.* Even if you are using a design agency or software package to create your Web site, you can still add HTML commands directly to your site.

For more information on HTML commands and meta-tag instructions consult the appendix.

Useful Web building sites

There are many sites that can help you decide which Web design option will be best for your company. Here are some of them:

■ *Builder* (*www.builder.com*) (see Figure 3.1). Billed as 'The Site for Site Builders', Builder provides features and workshops on

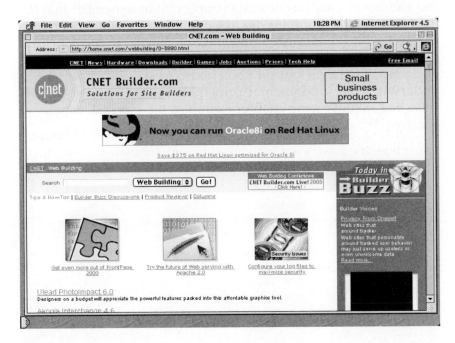

Figure 3.1 Builder Web site. Builder provides useful features on effective Web design

successful site design as well as links to helpful design tools. Whether you are a Web design virgin or veteran this site will help you work at your own level.

- *About (www.webdesign.about.com).* This site has done the hard work for you as it provides links to a wide variety of articles at different design sites.
- *Developer (www.developer.com).* This is where you go to find out technical information: its content includes advice on programming and HTML. Although the information is aimed at technophiles a lot of the articles are very accessible.
- *Internet Works (www.iwks.com).* As well as providing useful features on Web site design this site also provides a comprehensive directory of UK-based Web design firms.

Summary

Once you have formed a plan of what you want your Web site to achieve, your next step is to decide how to build your site. Your decision will be based on various factors including time, money and the size of your business. It is important to remember that the three Web building options discussed in this chapter are not mutually exclusive. For instance, knowledge of HTML can prove helpful even if you use a Web design agency or a Web building software package. Whichever option you choose, it will be important to understand the fundamental principles behind successful Web sites, and the following chapter examines the essential aspects of effective Web design from an e-marketing perspective.

four

Web design
principles

Although there are thousands of places you can go to find out about the technical aspects of Web site design (the appendix of this book being one of them), it's rare to find a useful source of information on what actually constitutes a good commercial Web site. In part, this is due to the fact that Internet companies themselves have often been too focused on technology at the expense of the human experience involved when people arrive at a site.

As Intel chairman Andy Grove has observed, e-businesses spend a lot of time thinking about what computers can do, but not much time thinking about what people can do with them. 'Fancy features may attract attention to a Web site' he comments, 'but they're no substitute for understanding customers or for human relationships.' The emphasis on technology over psychology may be attributable to the fact that the Internet is still a relatively new media form.

Problems occur when technology is seen as important in its own sake. Many Web sites have failed because they have valued fancy graphics and technical features above human interaction. Companies that have launched million-dollar Web sites, and which have been bolstered by multi-million dollar marketing campaigns, have failed to achieve repeat traffic because they have built a site from a technological rather than human perspective.

Back to basics

One of the most important consequences of the collapse of many high-profile dot coms has been a back to basics rethinking of what actually constitutes a good Web site. Of course, this may end up being as futile a question as what makes a good business or even how long is a piece of string, but there remain lessons to be learnt from the Internet fallout. One emerging consensus of opinion is the understanding that good Web site design is more than a question of aesthetics.

There is a fundamental difference between a good-looking site and a good site. Boo.com, for instance, was a visually attractive site yet poor navigation and usability meant it was ultimately doomed to failure. On the Internet, beauty is only screen-deep and not a solid enough basis for a long-term relationship with a target audience. From Amazon.com to eBay, the Internet success stories are surviving on more than their looks alone. To succeed in cyberspace Web sites need to match style with substance by taking the Internet on its own terms.

The purpose of this chapter then, is to look at the human principles of Web site design, so that your site will enable you to build mutually beneficial long-term relationships with your target audience.

Six general principles

The key to effective e-marketing is individuality. To talk about one type of successful site is therefore impossible: what works for one business may well not work for another. The Web would certainly be a worse place if every site followed the same uniform pattern. That said, there are general principles which can apply to all sites, and which in fact encourage individuality.

1. Identify your audience

Who are you designing for? Are you designing for a clearly defined niche audience or a broad cross-section of Internet users? Is it a domestic or international audience that you are targeting? The answers to these questions will help determine the design of your site. The more specific the target audience the more you will be able to fine tune the information on your Web site.

2. Make a good first impression

The first page a visitor arrives at is likely to be the one that makes the greatest impression. Minimal text, simple (and not too many) links as well as a speedy download time are essential first page ingredients.

3. Keep your site up to date

A week may be a long time in politics but it is a lot longer in cyber-space. Internet time is believed to move at seven times the velocity of normal time. Many people who *browse* (don't be fooled by this leisurely verb) the Internet return to the same sites every day. Information needs to be updated at regular intervals to keep a Web site fresh.

4. Satisfy itchy fingers

Goldfish are said to have an attention span of five seconds, which is approximately two seconds longer than visitors to your site. If they are visiting your site via a search engine, they may have up to 10 other sites they want to visit before they log off. The trick is to make your design stimulating while keeping it user-friendly. Slow down-load times, repetitive text and lengthy e-commerce processes must therefore be resisted.

5. Keep it human

Claude Levi-Strauss, the French anthropologist, refers to *bricolage* as the opportunism of those who work with their hands, creating things out of whatever is lying around. The Web works the same way: there is no set way of designing a Web site. Designers cut and paste tried and tested images, formats and links from each other to create new pages. According to *The New York Times'* David Weinberger, 'this makes the Web unpredictable, creative and always the result of human hands'.

6. Be proud to be imperfect

Due to its vast, complex and decentralized nature the Web will, in the words of Tim Berners-Lee, its inventor, 'always be a little bit broken'. The Web's frailty makes it more human and also renders the pursuit of perfection impossible. As Mark Gransee, Vice President of Information Systems at Eddie Bauer said (in a recent *Information Week* article) 'you just have to do the best you can!' The politics of 'being right' must not therefore be transferred to your Web site; rather, the aim should be to start a two-way conversation with your target audience, rather than to tell them, 'This is how it is.'

User-friendly sites

If people find it difficult to use your site, they are unlikely to make a return visit. Although it is important that your site is visually attractive, it is even more essential that visitors find their way around with ease. Here are some guidelines Web designers follow when creating user-friendly sites.

Keep it simple

Keeping it simple is perhaps the most important rule of Web site design. However, it takes a lot of time and effort to keep things as straightforward as possible from a visitor's perspective. Stephen Freeman, creative brain for retail.co.uk draws attention to this paradox. 'Simple isn't easy', he says. 'Sites that are overly confusing and filled with flashing gizmos that perform clever tricks without rhyme or reason are the ones which were created in an afternoon.'

Make links clear

Part of keeping it simple involves making sure your links are clear. Avoid using clever icons for links when a word would do. 'Home', 'News', 'Contact' and 'About this site' may seem slightly dull titles for links but they will be instantly recognizable to your visitor. Links should also be kept towards the centre of the page so that visitors don't have to scroll down or across to reach them. Tas Hajisavva from Get Tracking offers this advice: 'Make sure the links are not entirely alien to the site visitor; if it is hard work to find your way around a Web site it is unlikely you will return.'

Use straightforward navigation

There are a number of ways you can make it easy for people to find their way around your site. One way is to make sure no page of your Web site is further than three clicks away from any other. Another is to tell people where they are. You can do this by providing a site map or by changing the colour of the current section in the navigation area. A clear and self-explanatory home page also aids navigation.

Be familiar

With over a billion Web pages out there, it is unlikely you will be able to come up with a concept that is completely new. In fact, this may be a good thing. Web users like familiarity, they like to be able to recognize what they are expected to do.

Get to the point

A commercial Web site should make its intention clear from the outset. The home page should include enough information about your site and company to let visitors know if they have found the right place.

Consider download times

Lots of big or intricate images should also be avoided as they take time for visitors to download. Use spot graphics (small images) or images with minimal detail as they download quicker.

Avoid unnecessary forms

This is especially important if you have an e-commerce site, as extensive form filling can complicate the e-shopping experience. One solution, if you have the resources, is to store information (credit card details, customer preferences, etc) so that visitors only have to fill in forms on their first visit. While this tends to involve using expensive software, there are other ways to simplify the e-commerce process such as isolating order buttons.

Sites for sore eyes

The visual appearance of a Web site depends entirely on the objectives you want it to achieve. For information-rich sites the emphasis should be on straightforward navigation rather than fancy graphics. Think of how Yahoo! and other portals present their information. If, however, your main objective is to consolidate your brand identity it may be more appropriate to limit the amount of text on the site and concentrate on the graphics. When you are considering the visual dimension of your Web site you must acknowledge that a Web site is not a fashion statement, but the starting point for your relationship with a target audience.

Other, more specific, areas you should consider in relation to the visual appearance of your site include the following.

Banner advertising

Selling banner advertising on your site can be a great source of additional revenue, but it can lead to design problems. Banner ads can weaken the coherence of your brand message, especially if the advertising company doesn't fit well with your site. Furthermore, banners have a tendency to be garish and multi-coloured. This is because advertisers have to grab the attention of your site's visitors with a very limited amount of space. As well as garish colour schemes, banners often use animated graphics that can also damage the visual consistency of your site.

Images

Images are an obvious way to liven up a Web site. Too many, however, can detract from the information your site contains. Always try to use images to support and add value to your text as opposed to the other way around. Furthermore, although Web browsers support both GIF and JPEG files (two image formats), GIF files are quicker to download. JPEGs work better for photographs, however.

Browsers

Different Web browsers display information in different ways. Colour schemes, font sizes, text emphasis and other visual elements can all appear differently. Make sure you check the appearance of your Web site on different browsers as it is being designed.

Animation

Animated graphics can help keep your site visitors stimulated, but too many colours can cause annoyance. Limit animated images to a maximum of one per page.

Colour

A busy, kaleidoscopic site will end up giving your visitor a migraine, and migraines won't help you get your message across. Cleaner sites with a minimal and coherent use of colour (stick to two or three dominant colours) make a better psychological impression. Dark multi-coloured interfaces and two-tone backgrounds can make text difficult to decipher. As Web Guru Peter Kent rightly comments, 'If two-tone backgrounds are such a good idea, don't you think the world of print would have adopted them by now?' However, some colour combinations do work well on the Web. Gold on blue, for instance, provides a high level of contrast and can be used successfully to present information. The 'rainbow effect' created by too many or mismatched colours should be avoided as it causes your visitors confusion and eyestrain. Two or three dominant colours on your site are plenty if you want to create a clear and tasteful brand identity.

The main thing to remember when designing your Web site (or instructing a Web design agency) is not to get carried away. Restraint is the ultimate virtue when it comes to creating a site, although to look at many commercial Web sites you might not think it.

As Web software has developed over the years, many Web designers have felt the urge to demonstrate all these advances simultaneously on one Web page. Multiple animated GIF images, blinking text, Java script status bar messages, rainbow-coloured divider bars and pop up windows all on one screen may signify hard work on the part of the designer but will also result in hard work on the part of the site user.

Interactive designs

In the real world people *watch* TV, *read* the paper or *listen* to the radio.

These are all relatively passive activities. On the Internet, however, people *use* information. They are therefore involved with the messages they receive at a much deeper level. While viewers watch a 30-second TV ad they have no direct involvement, but when they spend 10 minutes making their own way through a Web site they interact with and become involved in the message. As solid and long-lasting relationships depend on interaction, the Internet can bring companies closer to their customers (and other audiences) than ever before.

The higher the level of interaction, the stronger the relationship. Amazon.com, arguably the world's strongest e-brand, encourages interactivity at every level, and even incorporates the user's voice into its media in the form of reader's reviews and rankings. Companies on the Internet are now moving away from brand breadth and starting to think about brand depth. In other words they are becoming less concerned about constantly finding new visitors, and are more interested in how to add value to their relationships with existing customers. This is leading to a move towards a cost-effective form of e-marketing based around the ultimate Web design principle: interaction. Here are some features that can add interactivity to your Web site:

Chat rooms

Chat rooms provide the most immediate sense of interactivity, as they enable people to communicate with each other instantly. For chat rooms to work, however, they need to be carefully monitored and you have to be sure that you attract enough visitors to make a chat room worthwhile. Generally speaking, chat rooms tend to work better on B2C (business-to-consumer) sites than on B2B (business-to-business) sites. To set up a chat room you will need, of course, special software such as Ichat (www.ichat.com) or ChatWare (www.eware.com).

Conference areas

Conference areas are the B2B equivalent of chat rooms. They enable companies to conduct business meetings, live seminars and press conferences from their Web site. Conferencing software is available from Proxicom (www.proxicom.com).

Guest books

Guest books provide a simple way of adding an interactive dimension to your site. They also provide your company with an effective feedback mechanism. Although they serve a similar function as a bulletin board (see below) they are a lot easier to manage once incorporated on your site. Your ISP will probably be able to provide you with an interactive guest book facility at minimal expense.

Bulletin boards

Many successful community focused sites provide their visitors with bulletin boards where they can post messages to other members of the group. Bulletin boards provide an effective way of building one-to-one and one-to-many relationships, as well as giving people an incentive to return to your site. Furthermore, if you are planning to include a discussion group on your site, you will need to use bulletin board software as a starting point. A vast and diverse range of bulletin board software is available free from freeware sites such as Freecode (www.freecode.com).

Contact lines

Another way to deepen the level of interactivity at your site is to provide an interactive contact line, such as a help or advice line.

If you want to increase the interaction between your site and its visitors even further you could actually get people to contribute to the development of your site's content. This could be done either by encouraging your visitors to send you articles, reviews and features (like Amazon does) or by asking their advice on how the site as a whole should move forward.

Avoiding 'information overload'

While Internet users log on to retrieve useful information, they do not want to be burdened with screen after screen of unbroken text. Information therefore needs to be presented in an accessible and user-friendly way, which doesn't require too much effort on the part of the site visitor. One of the most common criticisms levelled at the Internet is that it takes people ages to find the information they have logged on to look for. If you can help people in their quest to find useful and relevant information you are almost guaranteed to generate repeat visits.

To present information effectively:

- *Use 'text-bites'.* By breaking up text into short bite-sized chunks, divided by frequent sub-headings, net users will be able to scan the screen for information of use to them.
- *Link to more in-depth material.* Make sure that users can decide what they want to know more about by providing links at the foot of text-bites.
- *Add a search facility.* If your site consists of more than 30 or so pages you should consider adding a search facility to your site. This will enable visitors to conduct keyword searches to find the information they want.
- *Make use of white space.* Having plenty of white spaces, or any spaces without text or images, makes information easier to read on screen. Spaces give visitors a visual break and can draw them more easily to specific elements on a Web page.
- *Keep information fresh.* If you do not have the time to supply a fresh stream of information, or it simply seems like too much hard work, you could always hire a company to supply you with suitable content. Syndicated content is becoming increasingly popular with e-commerce sites wanting to provide their visitors with a one-stop information shop. The way it works is simple: you pay a company (such as the US-based Screaming Media) for a news feed and they provide you with up-to-date stories relevant to your site. No matter how 'niche' your online audience is, content providers will be able to supply the relevant information.
- *Use a suitable font.* The type of font you use can also make a big difference. The most popular real world font, Times Roman, does not transfer that well to the Web as its complex little flourishes are lost on Web pages. It's best to stick to clean fonts such as Arial, Helvetica or Verdana (which was designed specifically for the Web).

With regards to the words themselves, remember to resist the language of advertising. The Web should be seen as a worldwide conversation where the truth will always be outed. As Rick Levine of

Sun Microsystems has put it, 'Word of Web will trump word of hype every time.' Successful e-marketing therefore depends on discarding the language of advertising and embracing the word of Web. The fatuous self-praise which so often permeates company brochures and press releases must therefore be resisted, in favour of comprehensive, unfiltered information.

Designing from the outside in

Ultimately, if businesses are to take the Internet on its own terms, the provision of relevant information is essential. In the past, commercial Web sites have largely fallen into two, equally unsatisfactory, categories, which have taken as their inspiration outmoded real world templates. They have resembled either brochures or catalogues, and therefore left consumers with little incentive to log on.

Increasingly, however, e-businesses are taking the cyber-bull by its horns and looking at things from the site user's perspective. This 'outside in' approach not only helps the online consumer, but also instils in them the extra confidence needed to make a purchase.

By integrating your product or service details into something more informative, you will be able to join this new breed of e-business and realize your full online potential.

A creative approach

As differentiation holds the key to e-marketing success, it is important to take a creative approach to designing your Web site. After all, if your site fails to capture your own imagination it is unlikely to catch anyone else's. Having one unique feature which people will either find useful or entertaining will help keep your site in the minds of your audience. It will also give people a reason to talk about your site both online and offline. Furthermore, a unique design feature can also provide you with the hook needed to catch the attention of Web-weary journalists. Here are some diverse examples of unique and often quirky features on various successful sites to get you thinking.

Guinness: Boss Panic Button (www.guinness.com)

Guinness provoked a lot of interest in its Web site when it added a 'Boss Panic Button.' As Guinness had discovered that a lot of people visited its site during working hours, it decided to acknowledge this fact in the most novel of ways. If employees see their boss coming towards them, they can quickly click on the Boss Panic Button, which links to a very boss-friendly spreadsheet. The site subsequently received a lot of publicity in articles about the issues of Internet surfing at work.

Halifax: Mortgage Calculator (www.halifax.co.uk)

The Halifax Building Society's Web site includes a mortgage calculator, which enables visitors to work out what type of mortgage they are entitled to. This is an example of a site that enables visitors to personalize and interact with the information they receive.

Persil: Stains SOS (www.persil.co.uk)

The Web designers at Persil clearly conducted some lateral thinking when coming up with the Stains SOS section of this site. Obviously, the challenge they faced was thinking of a strong reason for people to visit the site that is still directly relevant to the product. The Stains SOS section provides information on different types of fabric stains and the best way to get rid of them.

Am I Hot or Not? The whole site (www.amihotornot.com)

Am I Hot or Not launched amid a blaze of free publicity in Autumn 2000, simply because it uses the interactive element of the Internet to come up with something completely different. The site enables people to put up a photo of themselves for other visitors to rate out of 10 (see Figure 4.1). Once you are at the site it is impossible not to get involved as to link to each page you have to give the present picture a rating. This site is a 'cruel but cool' example of how far a creative approach can get you on the Web. Set up on a shoestring

Figure 4.1 Am I Hot or Not? Web site. In this instance probably not

budget, the site now has visitors from around the world and a queue of sponsors knocking at the door.

Wedding Guide: Compatibility Test (www.weddingguide.co.uk)

This popular wedding portal incorporates a MENSA compatibility test, aimed to test out the strength of relationships scientifically.

The Ministry of Sound: VIP Room (www.ministryofsound.com)

This UK-based nightclub and 'youth lifestyle empire' replicates the nightlife experience on its Web site through its members-only VIP room. Once in the VIP room (which can be accessed by password only) members can chat to each other and download exclusive tracks from their favourite DJs.

Useful sites

As well as sites that can help you overcome your Web design dilemma (as detailed in the last chapter), there are also many that cover the essential principles of Web site design. Here are a handful of the best:

▨ *Web Sites That Suck (www.websitesthatsuck.com).* This site aims to 'teach good design by looking at bad design', providing links to sites that suffer from a variety of Web design disasters. It also provides you with a running commentary on just how and why those sites 'suck'.

▨ *.net Magazine Online (www.netmag.co.uk).* The online home of *.net* magazine includes a 'Web Builder' section full of Web design tips for the amateur and professional.

▨ *Alpha Project (development.alpha-project.net).* This site provides free online Web design tutorials.

▨ *Net B2B (www.netb2b.com).* The Net B2B site is full of useful articles on Web design from a business-to-business perspective.

▨ *Tips and Tricks (www.tips-tricks.com).* As its name suggests this site provides plenty of 'tips and tricks' on designing Web sites. It also provides lots of useful links to other Web design sites.

▨ *User Interface Engineering (www.uie.com).* Provides more advanced technical information on the principles and practice of Web site design.

▨ *Wilson Web (www.wilson-web.com).* Although this site is devoted to every aspect of Internet marketing, it provides particularly useful information on Web site design. There's also an e-marketing newsletter you can subscribe to.

Summary

Web sites are not simply intended to look pretty, they are expected to *do* something. It is therefore essential that when you design your site you remember that form follows function. As the design principles touched upon here have hopefully made clear, successful Web sites are always designed with the end user in mind. This 'outside in' approach will help you meet online marketing objectives and build long-term relationships with your audience. The guidelines detailed in this chapter are not set in stone; they are intended to inspire rather than confine you as you create or redevelop your site.

five

Search **engines**

Search engines have a vital role to play in any Web site's marketing activity. There are over 1500 search engines on the Web, although the majority are quite small and some of the largest search engines share the same databases. Most search engines are free to subscribe to and are, in effect, a worldwide free advert for your company. Although an estimated 80 to 85 per cent of Web users use search engines as a tool of first resort, most only look at the initial search results. It is therefore not just about registering with a search engine and hoping for the best: the aim is to ensure that your site ranks high (ideally in the top 20) when a relevant keyword is typed. This is no mean feat as different search engines use different criteria to rank Web sites and often try to keep their searching policies secret. However, as this chapter will explain, there are measures you can take to ensure that your site is search engine friendly.

Preparation

The large search engines have high standards and the sophisticated nature of the spiders that scour the Internet looking for new Web sites to appear on their sites means that even without the aid of human discretion they will be able to judge the quality of your Web site. Before you submit your site to the search engines you therefore have to make sure it will make the grade. To make your site search engine friendly you will need to follow the guidelines outlined below.

Obtain your own domain name

As well as registering your business name you could also try to get a domain name that includes a word that may be searched for.

Registries are now able to register domains of up to 63 characters providing businesses with more opportunity to include keywords in their Web site name. When searching for alternative, keyword-based domain names, visit Nameboy (www.nameboy.com) which checks out the availability of a domain name based on a keyword selection.

It is a lot easier to make an impact on the major search engines if you have your own domain name. Owning a domain name communicates your commitment to your site in a way that having a free site hosted by your ISP (Internet Service Provider) does not. Web sites that are located on free Web spaces do not fare well and in fact some search engines reject them instantly. The address, www.mysite.com would therefore be given preference over www.demon.net/mysite.

Design your site with search engines in mind

Page design is an important factor in ensuring a good search engine position. The search engines are not interested in the aesthetics of your site: they are looking at information and the way that information has been presented. If you are designing your Web site for search engine approval, you should:

- *Avoid too many graphics.* A graphics-heavy home page can put the search engine 'robots' off.
- *Check links.* Links that lead to an out-of-date URL can easily be checked by search engines, so be careful.
- *Make sure your site is compatible with most browsers.* Checking your site from different browsers will help you make sure it looks good to visitors and search engines alike.
- *Keep frames to a minimum.* Avoid frames because search engine robots cannot read them.

Get your meta-tags right

Meta-tags are HTML instructions that contain your keywords and help search engines index your site. Without meta-tags every single word on your site will be treated as a keyword. All the main search engines rely, in part, on the meta-tag to effectively categorize your site.

Due to the sheer number of sites on the Web, search engines have to automate the process of indexing sites. To do this they send out their robots to trawl through the Web on the lookout for new sites. Robots rely on these special meta instructions embedded into the head part of your Web site's HTML code. There are two main types of meta-tags: the description tag and the keyword tag.

This is an example of how meta instructions are laid out:

```
<Head>
<Title> My home page </Title>
<META name = "description" CONTENT = "A description of your Web
    site goes here">
<META name = "keywords" CONTENT = "a, list, of, keywords, and,
    relevant, phrases, goes, here">
</Head>
```

The description meta-tag

The description tag allows you to provide a 15–25 word description of your site, which will appear on search engine displays. Meta descriptions should give a general flavour of what visitors can expect from your site or page without burdening them with too much information. Take time to think of a good description, because you will be able to use it again when you submit your site to the search engines (remember meta-tags are for when search engines come to you). This is LetsBuyIt.com's description tag:

<META name="description" CONTENT="LetsBuyIt.com uses the principle of co-buying to drive prices down. Our members use collective intelligence and group buying power to reduce the cost of a wide range of consumer and business products.">

The keywords tag

The keywords tag lets you enter a list of relevant keywords for your site. You do not need to incorporate these tags on every page, but you should definitely add them to your home page and on main pages. This is an example of Last Minute.com's keyword tag (note that LastMinute.com includes different language keywords to cater for its international audience):

<META name="keywords" CONTENT="Flights, cheap flights, tickets, last minute, lastminute, last minute holidays, late bookings, holiday deals, lates, travel, holiday bargains, city breaks, deals, late-availability, late booking, package holidays, holiday deals, paris, eurostar, british airways, virgin, lufthansa, alitalia, continental, paris, venice, new york, boston, miami, barbados, london, hotels, travel

agent, travel agency, holiday flights, bargain holidays, vacation, trip, destination, airline, plane, discount, fares, savings, booking, ski holidays, alpine, tourismus, touristik, reise, flugverkehr, fluglinie, flughafen, urlaub, verreisen, reisen, fähren, fyndsemestrar, fyndflygresor, eating, restaurant, restaurants, london, food, wine, drinking, dining, dinner, supper, lunch, london restaurants, uk restaurants, food and drink, eating-out">

Establishing which words people would type into a search engine to find a site like yours can prove a difficult task, as there is often a limitless range of possibilities. Have a brainstorming session with colleagues or employees to come up with the words and phrases that you believe people looking for a site like yours would type into a search engine. Keep in mind that research has shown that 80 per cent of searches are done via phrases and not individual words. When writing keywords think about the words your target audiences would be likely to type in to find a site like yours.

If you are struggling with your keywords there is online help out there. There are a number of sites that help you refine your keyword selections. Good Keywords (www.goodkeywords.com) will help you find all the relevant keywords related to a primary keyword. For the phrase 'Web site design' it returns over 100 variations, each with the number of times it has been searched on. As an added bonus, when you have decided on your list, this site also creates the meta-tag for you to cut and paste into your Web page. A similar service can be found on the GoTo Web site (www.goto.com). At this site you can enter a keyword and find out which other words are most associated with it in searches. Once you have a keyword/phrase list the next step is to test them out at a main search engine. Try to avoid using keywords that are returning high matches: it's hard to come in the top 20 when you are competing with hundreds and thousands of other firms.

If you want a search engine to ignore a specific page for whatever reason, put the following meta command in the head section of the relevant page(s):

<META name = "robots" CONTENT = "No index, no follow">

To view a site's meta-tags go into your site and click on 'Source' then 'View'. The HTML text (including the meta-tags) will then appear on the screen. A good tip is to look at the meta-tags of sites that rank high on search indexes to get an idea of the sort of keywords and descriptions that work.

It is perfectly possible to build a site and ignore these meta-tags as they do not alter or affect what the visitor sees. However, if you are concerned about being included on search engines (and you should be) you need to treat meta-tags with the respect that they deserve.

More meta-tag information can be found in the appendix of this book.

Concentrate on quality

Increasingly, search engines are following Yahoo!'s lead and supplementing technology by employing panels of experts to rank sites on the basis of quality. At Lycos, for instance, a team of human experts are responsible for choosing the first 10 results in a search. The next three results are determined by the popularity of sites, and the remainder are based on keywords in a site found by Lycos's robot.

The major search engines exist to provide a worthwhile service to people searching at their sites. It therefore doesn't matter how many tricks you use to get your site ranked in a preferential position, if your site doesn't make the grade you have little chance of being indexed.

Refresh your site

As people are more likely to come back to a site that is updated, search engines rank regularly refreshed sites higher than those with unchanging content.

Include keywords in the body of your page

You should incorporate keywords into the main body of your text as well as in meta-tags and page titles. Most search engines take into consideration the first 150–250 words of your site, so your home page should be peppered with the words and phrases you use in your meta-tags. Make sure, however, that the keywords you use don't look forced or out of place. Not only will this damage the quality of your site but also search engines will discriminate against any site that lists keywords just for the sake of a high ranking. As Andrew Starling of *Internet* magazine advises, 'Three mentions in the first 150 words is ok. More can be self-defeating.'

Use the image and link tags

All images and links should have their own tags and ideally a keyword within them. Don't overdo this though as search engines may see it as 'spam indexing'.

Get the title tag right

The 'title' tag is not called a meta-tag, although it functions in a similar way. Search engines value the words in the title tag as more significant than any other words in your HTML text, excluding meta-tags. In fact, some search engines (of which AltaVista is one) can narrow searches down to an index of just page titles.

The rules for title tags are as follows:

- Make sure every page has a title tag. Unlike meta-tags, title tags are visible to your visitors and so omitting a title tag is a mistake that will not go unnoticed.
- Keep titles short. I would recommend a maximum of seven words.
- Make titles descriptive. There are two reasons for this. The first is that descriptive titles will help move search engines traffic towards your site. The second is that however long a page takes to load, the title loads almost instantaneously. Visitors with more lethargic Web connections can therefore get an indication of whether your site is for them before the page appears.
- The title tag should be readable and written in plain English, not just a list of keywords (but try not to use *or*, *and* and *the* too much).

Get some help

If the idea of being solely responsible for your HTML and meta-tags is daunting, there is help out there. Meta-tag services and advice can be found at the following URLs:

Web site Promote (www.websitepromote.com)
Northern Webs (www.northernwebs.com)
Site Up (www.siteup.com)

As well as getting general keyword advice it is also possible to analyse your own meta-tags at Web site Garage (www.websitegarage.com; see Figure 5.1) and Siteowner (www.siteowner.com).

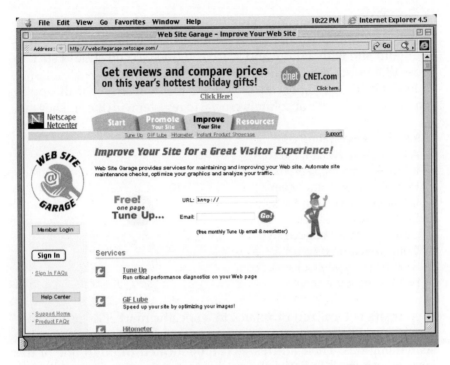

Figure 5.1 The Web Site Garage Web site. Web Site Garage can provide you with a meta-tag MOT

How to register with search engines

Although, in theory, you can wait for the search engine 'robots' to pay your site a visit, if you want to make sure it is considered for submission, your site will need to be registered. There are various ways to register your site with the major search engines. The most obvious, although also the most time-consuming, involves registering each site manually.

Manual registration

You can visit each search engine individually and manually fill in an electronic registration form on each one. If you register manually you can tailor the information to each individual search engine and each audience that uses each search engine.

If you choose to register your site by hand, you will have to decide which sites are worth the effort. Obviously it is impractical to register your site with a thousand search engines so you should stick to those that your target audience are most likely to use.

In all likelihood 95 per cent of your visitors will arrive via the top 10 search engines, so it's absolutely crucial to register with them. They are:

Yahoo! – www.yahoo.com
AltaVista – www.altavista.com
Infoseek – ww.infoseek.com
Hotbot – www.hotbot.com
UK index – www.ukindex.co.uk
Excite – www.excite.com
Google – www.google.com
Goto – www.goto.com
Looksmart – www.looksmart.com
Lycos – www.lycos.com

If your site is localized or relates to a specific market or profession, remember also to register your site with relevant market-specific search engines. Their addresses can be located through one of the large search engines listed above.

Yahoo! site submission

Submission Page: www.yahoo.com/info/suggest/

Yahoo!, the biggest and most popular search engine of them all, is the most important place for your site to get listed. The main Yahoo! Index is compiled by a staff of hundreds who assess each submission and decide whether it should be included in the directory. The staff can reject it if they personally do not feel the site is right for Yahoo! This means as well as a way of reaching your audiences, Yahoo! should be regarded as a human and subjective audience in itself. Owing to the complicated nature of its submission process and the fact that it is so important to get it right, it is worth concentrating on the specifics of registering with Yahoo! The other reason for focusing on Yahoo! is that, once you have mastered the Yahoo! registration method, you will be able to handle all the other search site submission forms with comparative ease.

Here are a few tips to make your site 'Yahoo! compatible':

- As Yahoo! is a directory it indexes sites by characters, not words, try and make sure your site title's first letters are from the beginning of the alphabet. If you have more than one domain name, and one begins with the letter D and the other with the letter P, it is therefore better to register the one beginning with D.

- Your site description should be between 25 and 35 words. Your site will have more chance of being indexed if you try and use as many keywords as possible and limit the amount of conjunctives.
- Go to your chosen category and choose the 'Add URL' button at the bottom of the screen. This will let Yahoo! know that you have submitted your site manually (automated submissions are often rejected by Yahoo!)

Here is a blow by blow account of the lengthy Yahoo! registration process:

- Go to the category you want be listed under. If you are unsure perhaps you could type in some of your competitors' names and see what category they are listed under. Submit your site for easy Yahoo! categories, not difficult ones. It's far easier to get into a regional Yahoo! category than the main international (predominantly US) area. (It's also easier to get into the personal page sections than in the business listings.) When choosing your category try and choose one with as few entries as possible.
- Click on the 'Add URL' icon at the bottom of the page. This will take you to the relevant submission page.
- Write the name of your company and Web address.
- Add keywords that are comparable to index headings or topics. For instance, if you sell mountain climbing equipment you could list words such as mountain, climbing, sports, outdoors, travel, exercise, hiking, absailing and so on.
- Provide a 20-word description of what your company does.
- Select the category you want to be listed in (for example, 'Business_and_Commerce: Public Relations Agencies.')
- Submit your name and e-mail address.
- Click on the 'submit' button.
- You will receive confirmation by e-mail.
- Resubmit your site into additional categories. This is especially beneficial if you sell multiple products.

Yahoo submissions take between two and eight weeks to appear. If your site is not on the index within eight weeks you will probably

need to register your site again. It can often take as many as 10 submission attempts before your site is accepted for indexing.

Submission programs

If you are put off by the idea of manual registrations you may be
tempted to use an automated program which will register your site
automatically. While this may be the most attractive option, it may
not be the most successful. The problem with submission programs
is that they have a tendency to view all the search engines as equal. If
you use an automated program, you will only be asked for two
descriptions of your site (one short, one long).

There are many sites that will submit your Web site details for
free, such as Submit It! (www.submitit.com). However, as each individual search engine uses different criteria, the best results are
obtained by a careful choice of a title, effective use of keywords in
meta-tags, and therefore by submitting your site to each major
search engine individually. There is, however, a strong argument for
using free submission programs in conjunction with manual registrations. This way you can make sure you submit to the top 10 search
engines according to their specific criteria, while leaving the lesser
populated search sites to be handled automatically.

For other submission programs check out:

Exploit – www.exploit.com
Did It – www.did-it.com
All4one – www.all4one.com
Web Position Gold – www.webposition.com
Agent Web Ranking – www.aadsoft.com
Sign Poster – www.signposter.com

Another reason for considering free submission programs is that if
your site fails to get indexed on a particular search engine, it will
automatically resubmit it until it does.

Web positioning firms

Owing to the fact that a lot of firms find the whole search engine
process arduous and time-consuming, a whole new industry has
emerged catering for companies' Web positioning requirements.

Many companies that rank high on the main engines, such as Intel, QXL and LastMinute.com, maintain their position by outsourcing to e-marketing firms that concentrate solely on search engines. For instance, Jean-Pierre Eskenazi, chief executive of NetBooster, says his company is focused 100 per cent on manually registering a company's Web site on search engines. 'Our dedicated team keeps abreast of the many changes required by search engines for effective submission, and we guarantee our customers a high placement on search engines.' However, as more and more search engines are basing positions on human judgement, there is no way of ensuring a top ranking for the long term, even if you do hire the services of a Web positioning firm.

Pay and display

Until recently the major search engines did not offer their customers the choice of paying for search engine submission. Sites would only charge for banner ads to be displayed whenever someone typed in a relevant keyword.

The Californian dentist Harold Ganz, who specializes in halitosis, pays AOL and Yahoo! over $50,000 a year. For this he gets a banner ad every time the keywords 'bad breath', 'halitosis' or 'fresh breath' are typed in to the search engine. Now, however, many search engines are charging for sites to be included on the index itself. For instance Godado charges businesses to register on its search engine and, controversially, displays how much Web site owners have paid. Not all the major search engines offer payment schemes but below is some information on those that do.

Inktomi (www.inktomi.com)

Inktomi (the index that supplies data to HotBot, AOL, MSN and certain areas of Yahoo!), launched a system in late 2000 that guarantees site owners inclusion on its database if they pay a fee. Payment guarantees inclusion on their database within two days and confirms a Web site listing for a period of one year. However, although pages are guaranteed to be listed if you pay, your ranking is not. Inktomi is using the same process as before to rank sites. The company is phasing out the free 'Add URL' pages that are listed on its site because half of what it receives is spam, although it will still be sending out its spiders and pages will still be listed free this way.

The Inktomi order form is at www.inktomi.com/products/portal/search/pagesubmission.

Ask Jeeves (www.askjeeves.com – co.uk)

Ask Jeeves offers a paid inclusion programme called 'Answer Link', where Ask Jeeves is paid on the amount of traffic it sends to the customer's site. Customers cannot control exactly what questions their company will appear under because Ask Jeeves has to deem the site relevant. Ask Jeeves has a stringent policy of who it allows to use its inclusion scheme (only 5 per cent of its database is from paid inclusion) and your site has to be of a high quality. Sites that have made the list include GE Financial, All Business, On Health and Ticket Master. Policy information for the 'Answer Link' programme can be found at www.askjeeves.com/docs/about/policy.

Look Smart (www.looksmart.com)

Look Smart's paid inclusion programme is called 'Sub Site'. It works very much like Ask Jeeves's 'Answer Link' where all Web sites have to be verified by the editorial team before inclusion and customers pay by the 'click through' rate. The difference is that although the editorial team review your site in detail they also categorize individual pages rather than Web sites. Therefore Web sites could end up with hundreds of different listings. Also, Look Smart offers any Web site the opportunity to join its sub-site programme (provided the site meets its editorial standards). EBay is one of the sites that take advantage of this programme.

Go To (www.goto.com)

Go To offers something slightly different. Rather than operating a 'paid inclusion programme' it offers a 'paid placement program'. Placement programmes guarantee positions and if you want to be the number one search finding when somebody types in 'cheese', all you have to do is negotiate with Go To and pay for that privilege.

Cheating the search engines

Many companies still believe the best way to arrive at the top of the search engines is to cheat. While in the early days of the Web it was possible to get away with underhand methods, now the search engines all take a harder line. If you are caught in the act you are likely to be blacklisted, not only from that particular engine but also from all the major search sites and directories. The following methods should therefore be resisted at all costs:

- *Using unsuitable keywords.* Keyword combinations such as 'Triple X action' and 'free money' may get people to your site, but you need to remember that when it comes to site traffic, quality not quantity is important.
- *Using the same keyword more than once.* This used to be accepted practice. Now 'keyword stuffing' is frowned upon and the search engine robots trawling the Web looking for sites will deliberately ignore stacked keywords. However, it is perfectly acceptable to put different synonyms or related words in meta-tags such as 'PR, public relations, marketing, promotion, publicity'.
- *Stealing meta-tags.* Copying another site's meta-tag structure is illegal and is probably the most severe search engine sin of all. Many Web site owners have ended up in court as a result of meta-tag plagiarism.
- *Submitting different pages of the same file.* If a site has more than one page, it is not automatically expected to have more than one sub-mission.
- *Using multiple titles.* Search engines will only acknowledge one meta-tag title per page.
- *Incorporating competitors' names into meta-tags.* While it may seem logical to incorporate the names of competitors within a meta-tag (to catch visitors typing their names into a search engine), it is a breach of copyright.
- *Submitting different URLs of the same site.* Sites with more than one URL or Web site address may be tempted to pretend they are two separate sites. As soon as the search engine robot sees the iden-tical HTML script it will reject the submission.
- *Displaying an invisible line of keywords.* Displaying an invisible line of keywords with identical text and background colours will result in instant exclusion from most search sites.
- *Repeating keywords in the main text.* Repeating the same keywords more than five times on a page is also likely to get you struck off.
- *Spam indexing.* Don't use the same keywords for each doorway page. Search engines hate this and refer to it as spam indexing. Alta Vista claims that of the 20,000 subscriptions it receives per day, half are spam.

Evaluating your search technique

To see how successful your efforts have been, you can use a free online tool called Website-Rank (www.website-rank.com), which will tell you where your site is positioned on all the main search engines when people type in your keywords. You should monitor your ranking at least once a month as positions can change at break-neck speed as new sites are submitted and old ones updated.

There are other software products available which monitor how people arrive at your site. They not only tell you whether they used a search engine, but also which search engine they used and what keywords they typed in. See the concluding chapter for a more in-depth discussion of these products.

If your ISP can provide you with 'access logs' (records of your site's activity based on file requests) you will also be able to tell when a search engine robot or spider has visited your site, and even whether or not they have picked it up for indexing. If there are any requests for something called a 'robotz.textfile' it means a robot has conducted a 'reading' of your site. To find out which search engine the robot comes from you will need to be aware of the name of each site's robot. Here are the five main robots you are likely to encounter (they are listed next to the search engine they belong to):

Scooter (AltaVista)
Slurp (HotBot)
Architext (Excite)
Sideminder (Infoseek)
Gulliver (Northern Light)

A slow process

Although the Internet is a fast-moving medium, search engine registration is an unavoidably slow process. It often takes over a month, and various attempts, before the engine will list your site. If you still are not getting anywhere you may have to rejig your meta-tags, page titles and even content and then resubmit your site. It takes time but will eventually pay off. If you have confidence in your site, you shouldn't throw in the towel until you see it in the top 10 sites in each category you want to be listed under. When you are conducting repeat submissions it may be an idea to maintain a record of relevant information (such as which pages were submitted, which search engines they were submitted to and the submission date).

Summary

Search engines are the main tool people use to find where they are going online and to pull information towards them. Therefore not only is search engine registration essential, but you also need to ensure your site ranks highly when a user types in relevant keywords or phrases. To do this, you need to take time over your meta-tags and think carefully when you are filling in search site submission forms.

Furthermore, as search engines are increasingly using human judgement to rank sites, you also need to ensure the quality of your entire site is up to the specific engine's requirements. While it is possible to trick a robot over the content of your site, a human being will be harder to fool. The other point to remember is that search engines aren't an end in themselves. If a visitor reaches your site via a search engine and finds nothing of interest, he or she will click the 'back' button within a matter of seconds. In short, no matter how adept you are at form filling and at choosing keywords, if your site doesn't appeal at a human level it is unlikely to fulfil your marketing objectives.

More marketing **channels**

Although search engines look set to remain one of the most important means of channelling Internet users towards specific Web sites, they are by no means the only online routes to your home page. This chapter looks at some of the other marketing channels that can be used to move Web traffic in the direction of your site. This includes not only those tools and techniques that can generate awareness among new online audiences, but also those which can lead to return site visits. To start with we will look at links to your site, or more specifically reciprocal links, as these are fast becoming one of the most convenient and cost-effective means of attracting both virgin and veteran visitors to a Web site.

Reciprocal links

Most people arrive at Web sites via links. This can either be through a search engine link, a link embedded in an e-mail message, or a link from another site. It therefore stands to reason that the more links to a site, the more chances there are that new visitors will make their way to it. However, in order to gain relevant links, you will probably need to offer a link in return.

Many companies remain sceptical about adding links to other sites within their own Web pages as they feel it is providing visitors with a reason to leave. The fact is, however, that people are going to leave your site whether you incorporate external links or not. By clicking through to a site you have recommended, a visitor will be keeping yours in mind as he or she journeys around the linked site. Instead of viewing links as a reason for people to exit your site you should therefore consider them as an additional incentive for people to get there in the first place. Furthermore, by linking to other exceptional sites you will be adding to your credibility by way of association.

Here are some of the ways to find suitable link partners:

- *Visit trade organization sites.* Trade organization sites such as that of the PRCA (Public Relations Consultants Association, www.prca.org.uk) often include links to various sites within their industry. You could therefore approach not only the trade site itself, but also the site it has links to, if it already has links.
- *Conduct link searches.* AltaVista and a few other search engines enable you to conduct link searches, whereby you can type in a domain name and find all the links leading to it. This can help you find sites linking to your immediate competitors, and therefore sites likely to link to your home page as well.
- *Look for sites near to yours on search engines.* Sites listed near to yours on search engines are likely to attract a similar audience, and therefore could prove beneficial link partners.
- *'Information only' sites.* Sites that function as 'information providers' often have lengthy link pages. As they don't have any rival products or services to sell, they are also likely to be more receptive than your competitors to the idea of a reciprocal link partnership.
- *Visit award sites.* Speciality award sites that give awards to sites within your market sector are a great place to hunt out potential link partners. Most award sites include an archive list of previous award winners, which you can have a look through to see which sites are well matched with yours. Provided the award scheme is recognized and respected, this is also a good way to ensure that you only contact sites worthy of a link.

Once you have found sites that have a suitable and substantial audience profile, find the relevant e-mail addresses and contact names. The next step is to put together a tailored and individualized message for each site manager. If you give the impression that you are sending out a bulk e-mail you will not receive a good response. When you are writing each message get to the point in the first couple of sentences. Tell the recipient what you like about their site and why you want to link to it. Tell them also how a link from your site could prove beneficial. This will lead nicely into the reasons why the site you are contacting should link to your site. Make sure that you are giving the person you are contacting a genuine impression of your site and include a link to your homepage at the foot of the message. The other important thing to remember is not to overstate your case. The length of each e-mail, as always, should be kept to a minimum so that the user won't need to scroll down to read the whole message.

'Free-for-All' links

A less discriminate, although often easier means of gaining links to your site is to sign up with a 'Free-for-All' (FFA) link service. These provide link lists that anyone can join for no fee whatsoever. Using a service such as Linkomatic (www.linkomatic.com) you can submit your site to hundreds of free link pages at once. While this may help to increase the volume of traffic, however, it will not necessarily benefit your e-marketing efforts in the long term. Link lists are often home to sites that have been rejected by the major search engines, and turned to the link lists as a last resort. If you join an FFA list, your site could therefore be rubbing shoulders with dubious sounding sites with names like 'My Pet Tarantula' or 'Triple X Action'.

Although a few years ago FFA link pages were seen as helpful search tools, they are now generally considered to be a cyberspace dumping ground for obscure or dubious Web sites. Therefore, while any link to your site is going to increase the number of visitors you have, traffic generated via FFA services is not necessarily going to be relevant to your e-marketing interests.

Web rings

One of the easiest ways to gain reciprocal links with other like-minded Web sites is to join a Web ring. For the uninitiated, a web ring is an online 'linked community' of sites attracting similar audiences. This community forms a 'ring' because each participating site links to two other sites (the previous and next site taking part in the ring), rather than to every other participating site. Collectively the sites form a ring, and every individual site is a link in the chain. By clicking on the next link at each and every site visitors can end up, eventually, back where they started. Web rings can work better than a normal 'reciprocal link' partnership because, although they harness the power of hundreds of sites together, this power is not diluted by incorporating hundreds of links on each site. This means people are likely to link to your site even if they've never heard of it before. Furthermore, as each site in the link is related in some way, the people who have 'clicked through' a link to your site will be more likely to be interested in your site once they get there. Unlike the 'hit or miss' aspect of other commercial communities, Web rings enable you to capitalize on the marketing activity of other similar sites.

The most popular Web ring service is the US-based (but internationally focused) Web Ring (www.webring.org; see Figure 6.1). Web Ring manages around 70,000 rings with approximately 500,000 sites taking part. The service allows you to search through different rings and visit databases of each ring (to help you make an 'at a glance' judgement). You will need to look very carefully at the sites participating in each ring. If you see a ring suited to your audience you can then submit your site and, provided Web Ring considers your site suitable, join the ring. If, on the other hand, there are no existing Web rings suited to your site you could join forces with a few other sites and form your own Web ring. Step-by-step instructions for forming your own ring can be found at the Web Ring site.

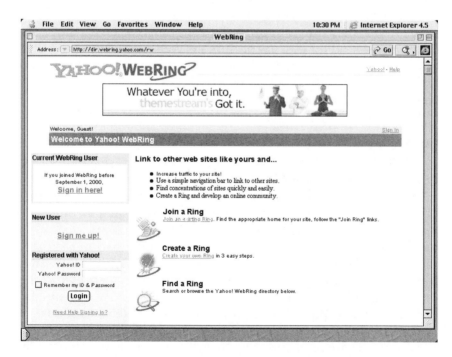

Figure 6.1 The Web Ring Web site. Web Ring is the most popular Web ring service

For further information on all aspects of Web rings, check out the following online resources:

Loop Link (www.looplink.com)
RainFrog (www.rainfrog.com)
Sadiq's Web Ring Directory (www.users.dircon.co.uk)

Relevant Web ring information can also be found at the following, somewhat long-winded, Yahoo! address: www.yahoo.com/computers_and_internet/internet/world_wide_Web/indices_to_Web_documents/rings.

Affiliate marketing

In July 1996, Amazon initiated a new way of marketing products via the Internet: affiliate schemes. This basically took the idea of link partnerships to a whole new level. Amazon decided that instead of just having sites linking to its home page, it would be a good idea to have other sites actually promoting and helping to sell its products. By offering sites a commission on products sold via this scheme, Amazon soon gathered an army of affiliates. Now Amazon has nearly half a million affiliates based all over the world.

The reason why this form of marketing can be so successful is because it benefits people on both sides of the affiliate coin. For the company setting up the scheme, it means an ever-expanding sales force that only gets paid if and when sales are actually made. The advantages for the site subscribing to the program are equally apparent. Sites receive commission without taking orders or delivering products, all of which remain the job of the site that set up the program and the software it uses. The only cost is the time it takes to find relevant affiliate merchants, link to them and then incorporate them on your site in a way that is likely to lead to sales. As a result of this win-win, minimum risk situation, affiliate marketing now accounts for around 25 per cent of all online spending, a figure which is growing exponentially.

Not all affiliate schemes are run in the same way as commission rates and the method of payment vary considerably. For instance, Amazon pays a fixed rate of 15 per cent on sales, whereas many of the major affiliate schemes (including CDNow's) work on an ascending scale. In other words, the more products each affiliate sells, the higher the commission becomes.

Setting up your own affiliate scheme

As more and more companies are looking towards the affiliate marketing model to generate more revenue and expand their customer base, setting up an affiliate scheme is becoming an easier task. While a few years ago it involved complex computer programming, the emergence of various affiliate software products has made affiliate schemes an option for virtually every e-commerce business. The most user-friendly packages provide a fully automated process, whereby everything from signing up new affiliates to commission tracking happens automatically. Some programs even let sites taking part in your scheme check on their sales statistics at your site. As well as software products there are also services available that will install the system on your server. More information on the various products and services can be found at Affiliate Zone (www.afiiliatezone.com) and Linkshare (www.linkshare.com).

Becoming an affiliate

If setting up an affiliate scheme yourself seems beyond your immediate capabilities, you could consider participating in someone else's program. By becoming an affiliate you can add another revenue stream to your online activity as well as enhance the end user's experience of your site. Although the process of becoming an affiliate is a relatively simple one (it often involves little more than cutting and pasting a chunk of HTML from the affiliate host), there are a number of issues to consider. The degree of success you have as an affiliate will depend on the following factors:

- *Suitability.* The more relevant the products you sell are to the content of the site, the easier it will be to convert site users into site customers.
- *The credentials of the company running the scheme.* The fact that you don't have to handle orders also means that you are putting the reputation of your site in another person's hands. It may even be worthwhile placing a few orders yourself before inviting your

site users to do the same. Trust takes time to build online and, when lost, can often be impossible to restore.

■ *The scale of your objectives.* Affiliate programmes can and do make money but they are rarely enough to financially support a Web site alone.

■ *The way the affiliate products are presented.* Affiliate partners are not offering their own, but someone else's products. To get people to buy products from your site rather than the affiliate host itself, you need to make sure they have a reason. For instance, they will be more likely to click and buy a book about vegetarian cookery if it follows a well-written and informative article on the subject.

■ *The payment deal.* The rate of commission ranges between 5 and 20 per cent.

Affiliate directories

Affiliate directories provide a mine of information for site owners wanting to sign up for affiliate schemes as well as for those looking to establish schemes of their own.

The directories enable you to link to sites that already take part in schemes so you can see how they work in practice. Some, such as the excellent Associate Programs site (www.associateprograms.com), hold their own discussion groups where you can ask questions on any area of affiliate schemes. Another directory, Site Cash (www.site-cash.com), rates sites on their ease of use providing a broad, comparative overview of all the different types of affiliate schemes there are. The Net Affiliate Scheme (www.netaffiliate.com) also provides a directory along with advice on how to choose the right programme for your business.

Web awards

There are literally thousands of award schemes on the Web, many of which can make a real difference to the number of visitors to your site. Whatever your site caters for, you can be sure that somewhere on the Web there is someone willing to endorse your efforts by offering an award. As well as a welcome pat on the back, winning an award can also help you achieve the following things:

- *Trust.* Award-winning sites are more likely to be trusted by potential e-shoppers as untrustworthy sites generally don't win awards.
- *Promotion.* Winning awards not only ensures promotion on the award site, but also increases your chances of publicity elsewhere.
- *Status.* Becoming an award-winner will enhance your site's status as a must-see site.

Of course, owing to the sheer number of award schemes out there many of them don't mean that much. There are, however, a number of Web awards that can probably add value to any site. These include *Project Cool* (www.projectcool.com), which was the first major Web award scheme, and Yahoo!'s 'Picks' awards. Being awarded as one of Yahoo!'s picks of the day means you will appear on one of the most visited Yahoo! pages. For a comprehensive list of Web awards visit Award Sites (www.focusa.com/awardsites), which also gives you an idea as to how valid each scheme is and how relevant it would be to your site.

Nominating your site for an award generally involves filling in a lengthy submission form. The sort of thing award givers are interested in include the popularity of your site, any other awards you might have won, search engine positions and any other unique features specific to your site. If you want to submit your site for lots of site awards simultaneously take a look at the Awards Jungle submission service (www.awardsjungle.com; see Figure 6.2), which does just that.

Announcing your site

If your site has just been developed, you should consider announcing the arrival of your site via one of the many announcement services that populate the Web. These are services solely devoted to 'getting the word out' about new sites; the most famous announcement service is probably Yahoo!'s What's New index.

Submitting your site to announcement services generally involves giving your Web site address along with a succinct description of what visitors are able to find at your site. This can be based on the site description you have submitted to the major search engines. This description will be read by people visiting each announcement

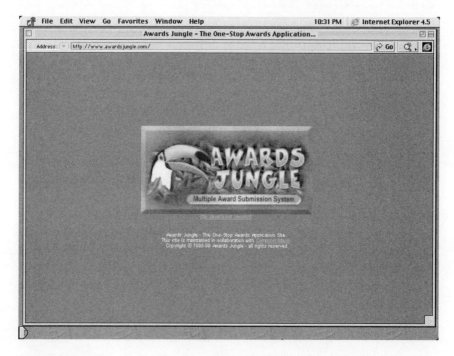

Figure 6.2 The Awards Jungle Web site. Awards Jungle's submission service will enter your site for many awards simultaneously

service so it should be clearly written and to the point. If you have no luck announcing your site the first time, most services enable you to have a second or third attempt. This means you can rework your site description a few times to see which version proves most successful. As well as Yahoo! you should also try the following popular announcement services.

- *Net Happenings (listserve.classroom.net)*. Although Net Happenings is a one-man operation, it has a huge reach. This is the service that distributes new site announcements via the thousands of discussion groups in Usenet as well as through a large mailing list. Although the submission procedure is rather lengthy and idiosyncratic, inclusion on the Net Happenings list means word of your site will reach a key population of committed net enthusiasts. These are the people who, via discussion groups and other channels, can create the sort of word of Web buzz some multinational companies would pay millions for.

- *Net Announce (www.erspros.com/net-announce).* Net Announce enables you to provide a more detailed description of your site than most of the other services. It does, however, have strict submission criteria that can be (perhaps deliberately) off-putting.
- *Netscape What's New (www.netscape.com).* Netscape offers a Yahoo! style What's New service, which is updated on a daily basis.
- *UK Index (www.ukindex.co.uk).* One of the main features of the UK index is its What's New directory, which is intended to announce new UK-based Internet companies.
- *Yellow Pages What's New (www.yell.co.uk).* The Yellow Pages' Yell Web site incorporates a What's New announcement section alongside its standard index. As with the main directory the What's New section is broken into different indexes based on different regions and then again into different business areas.

Announcement discussion groups

Although you have to be very careful when contributing to most online discussion groups in order to avoid being accused of 'spamming', there are a number of groups that welcome relevant site announcements. Unfortunately, there is no quick way of only searching through discussion groups that accept new site (or product) announcements. The only way you can do it is to visit Deja News (www.deja.com) and search through the 'biz.' (business and commercial) category of newsgroups. At a rough estimate, about one in every five biz newsgroups accepts, and is receptive to, new site announcements (provided of course that they are relevant to the newsgroup's current topic under discussion).

Building repeat traffic

Although it is important to raise awareness of your site among new audiences, you should not neglect to consolidate your site's profile among people who have already made the effort to seek you out. While a few years ago commercial sites simply played the numbers game, constantly thinking of ways to increase the number of people visiting their site, a shift of thinking occurred at the start of the new millennium. Now the emphasis is on increasing the 'lifetime value' of existing customers rather than on winning over first-timers. The reasons for this include the following:

- *Cost*. It generally costs less money to get people to return to your site than it does to boost awareness of your site among people who have never heard of you.
- *Conversion rates*. Research has shown that it is a lot easier to convert a repeat visitor into a customer, than it is to pull off the same trick with a 'newbie'.
- *Relevance*. Repeat traffic is increasingly valued above 'virgin visits' because people who decide to make return visits are generally more interested in your site than people who happen upon it by chance for the first time. Return visits are therefore more likely to fit within a relevant target audience.
- *Surfers*. Committed Web surfers (people who tend to visit lots of new sites regularly) are going to be less valuable to you than people who have a few regular sites they visit all the time. For regular visitors your site will constitute an end in itself, whereas for Web surfers it will be seen as just another click stop on their Web patrol.
- *Trust*. The more people visit a site the more they are likely to place their trust in it (provided, of course, the site deserves to be trusted). As we discuss elsewhere in this book, trust is one of the most important factors in getting people to spend money at a site.
- *Viral marketing*. Viral marketing is the term used to describe word of mouth publicity on the Internet. Word of mouth can spread *very* quickly online, via e-mail, Usenet discussion groups, chat rooms and so on. More often than not the topic of conversation revolves around Web sites, as people are often asking for recommendations of where to go or letting other people know about this great site they've visited. It almost goes without saying that people who have visited your Web site a number of times are more likely to tell other people about it than people who have only made one visit.
- *Branding*. As Matt Perry from Internet marketing firm Net Marketeers puts it, 'Repeat traffic builds brands. It's as simple as that.' The more people visit your site the stronger your unique brand identity becomes in their minds.

New content notices

Fresh content is *de rigueur* for your Web site if it is to attract repeat traffic. Static, unchanging sites (often referred to as 'cobweb' or 'wallpaper' sites) will inevitably prove to be one-click wonders and therefore should be avoided.

However, renewing your content on a regular basis is not enough in itself. You need to let people know that this new content is there. To do this you have several options:

- Mention new content in your e-mail newsletter.
- Send out separate e-mail notices to your mailing list.
- Add a 'Mind-It' form to your site. Mind-It is a feature available from the Net Mind site (www.netmind.com), which enables people to specify the changes they want to hear about, and then receive notice when these changes occur. The form can be incorporated anywhere on your site.
- Make it clear at your site which sections are updated and how often.

Tools for return visitors

While elsewhere in this book we will look at how community building is an effective way of ensuring that people will return to your site, you also need to look at the tools people use to return to a site.

Although search engines, announcement services and award schemes are great ways of generating fresh traffic, they are not so good at encouraging people to return. When people make a return visit to a site they don't always just type in the Web site address of the site in the browser. For instance, they often make a return visit via a link in an e-mail that had been sent out to them by the relevant Web site. In addition, people who like to visit the same sites again and again use four Web tools designed for the purpose: bookmarks, doorway pages, history lists and favourites lists.

Bookmarks

Both Netscape Navigator and Internet Explorer offer their users a wide range of popular bookmark tools. One of the most direct methods of generating repeat traffic is therefore to offer a friendly reminder to bookmark your site by placing a notice on each page saying 'Bookmark this site!' You could even provide information on how to use bookmarks. This can be a great way of compiling information with promotional content.

Doorway pages

If you use Netscape Navigator or Internet Explorer it is quite likely that their home page appears on your screen when you log on. However, both browsers enable users to use any other sites for starting, or, to use the right Web terminology, 'doorway' pages. If people used your page as their doorway page they would be reminded of your site each and every time they went online. Post a message on your home page asking people to change their starting page to yours, and offer them a reason why they should want to (if you are an e-commerce site you could offer daily discount coupons; if you are in the service sector you could use your useful 'tips of the day' as an incentive).

As people may not automatically know how to replace their start page, you should make sure that lack of knowledge will not prevent them, by providing the following guidelines:

- You can choose a new start page for your browser from the Internet Options box.
- To access the Internet Options box select 'View' then 'Internet Options'.
- Type the address (or URL) of the new home page into the Internet Options box.

Providing your site visitors with these instructions will benefit you in two ways. It will increase the chance of visitors making your page their starting page and it will help make your site a resource of valuable and objective Internet information.

History lists

A history list is a chronological record of visited web pages on your visitor's browser. It helps people visit sites they have forgotten to bookmark. To access the list they select 'Tools' then 'History', and then all they have to do is click on the address they want in the history list.

Internet users use history lists as a way of saving net-surfing time to visit sites they already know have proved useful to them before. The advantage history lists have over favourites lists (at least from the user's perspective), is that users can search the list by defining conditions such as 'Visit count is greater than 5'. This command would bring up only those sites they have visited more than five times. The different conditions relate to visit frequency, site size, as well as when the page was first and last visited.

To make sure your site continually comes up in history list searches you therefore need to make sure you not only generate repeat traffic, but also have lots of different web pages.

Favourites lists

The favourites list is available on both the main Web browsers (Internet Explorer and Netscape Navigator) as a convenient place in which to store Web addresses people might want to revisit. It allows users to return to a stored web site with a single click rather than having to type out the whole address. It can also serve to jog people's memory of useful sites they may have forgotten about. It can therefore provide people with a quick shortcut to your site. Many people, however, don't know how favourite menus work and often don't know they exist. It may prove beneficial to offer a helping hand at your site, so that your site will automatically become your visitor's first favourite. This will serve a dual purpose as not only will you be encouraging repeat traffic, but you will also be seen as a friendly source of Internet help. You could provide the following instructions:

- Favourite menus are accessed through Windows and Office programs.
- The command sequence is 'Start' – 'Favourites'.
- To add a web page to the menu then select 'Add to Favourites'.
- Enter the web site address in the dialogue box.
- To put the new favourite into a subfolder of the main folder, click the 'Create In' button and pick the subfolder into which you want to put the new favourite.
- To make a new folder for the favourite, select a folder in which to put the new folder and then click on 'New Folder'.

Summary

As the Internet is a 'pull' rather than a 'push' medium, you need to provide people with as many opportunities to pull your site towards them. The fact that there are so many Web sites out there (even, no doubt, within your specific sector) should therefore be seen less as a threat and more as a marketing opportunity. By partnering with other sites, either via reciprocal links or affiliate marketing schemes, you can benefit from their marketing and efforts in supplement to your own.

As well as providing many avenues to your site through your own initiatives, you should also think of actions your visitors can carry out in order to make it easier to return to your site. As more and more people are preferring to make repeat visits to sites they know and trust rather than risking venturing onto new ones, the use of Web browser tools such as bookmarks and history lists is on the increase. By reminding people of these facilities on your Web pages you will be helping people who already like your site to return on a regular basis.

Of course, as all of these techniques involve people coming to you, there is no way of making sure your marketing message will be heard by exactly the people you want to hear it. In order to be able to target people with an even greater degree of accuracy, you will therefore need to supplement the methods mentioned above with direct marketing activity, the subject of the next chapter.

seven

Direct
e-marketing

When most people think of the Internet, they generally think of Web sites. The fact remains, however, that Web sites are only one of the many e-marketing tools at a company's disposal. E-mail and newsgroups (either e-mail or Web-based) provide marketers with another, wholly different way to reach out to new prospects and consolidate relationships with existing customers. Whereas Web sites depend on people taking the effort or initiative to visit them, e-mail and newsgroups put the ball in the marketer's court by providing a means of contacting people directly. This chapter looks at the various ways the Internet can be used for direct marketing purposes as well as exploring the pitfalls that can be encountered.

The advantages of e-mail marketing

E-mail is increasingly seen as the ultimate direct marketing tool. When used responsibly, e-mail can achieve the kind of response only dreamt of in the days of more traditional forms of direct marketing. Its many advantages, for both companies and customers alike, include:

- *Cost.* E-mail is an inexpensive marketing tool when compared with more traditional methods such as posting mailshots or cold calling.
- *Immediacy.* As e-mail messages can be sent and received within seconds, e-mail provides immediate results.
- *Evaluation.* Due to the self-documenting nature of the Internet the results of an e-mail campaign can be measured down to the number of recipients who opened the message, clicked through

to the Web site, made a transaction or forwarded the message to a friend.

- *Availability*. E-mail messages can be sent or received at any time of day or on any day of the year. Furthermore, you can send as many messages to as many people as you want to, whenever and wherever you happen to be.
- *Environmentally friendly*. As the public at large views business attitudes towards the environment as increasingly significant, e-mail marketing can enhance your status as an environmentally friendly company. After all, the only resource e-mail uses is electricity.
- *Response*. Surveys have found that e-mail marketing campaigns can be as much as 10 times more likely to generate a response as their direct mail counterparts.

As Internet use continues to grow exponentially, the above advantages are starting to become ever more apparent and direct e-mail is increasingly taking precedence over traditional marketing methods.

E-mail marketing challenges

Although the many advantages of direct e-mail are undeniable, there are certain challenges e-mail marketers need to overcome. Primarily, Internet users are more and more sceptical about receiving any form of commercial message via e-mail. Outlined below are some related issues that need to be taken on board if you are going to use e-mail to maximum effect.

Spam

The term 'spam' now generally refers to unsolicited commercial e-mail (or UCE as e-marketing experts like to abbreviate it). This, however, can be a little misleading. For instance, if out of the blue an editor of a leading magazine sent you an e-mail asking to do a feature on your business or to have an interview with you, it is unlikely that you would consider the message spam (although it would be both unsolicited and commercial). Equally, if you sent a relevant and newsworthy media release via e-mail to a journalist you've never met before, you could, according to the strict 'UCE' definition, justifiably be accused of sending spam. Owing to the obvious weaknesses in the standard definition, Internet guru Peter Kent came up with a more useful definition of spam as 'unsolicited and indiscriminate bulk e-mail'. As Peter Kent himself explains in his *Poor Richard* guide to the Internet, there's a significant difference 'between buying millions of e-mail addresses on a CD and sending everyone a message asking them to visit your foot-fetish site' and 'carefully selecting a number of Web site owners who might want to review your product and mailing them all a polite message suggesting this'. While this is undeniably the case it is important to remember that spam is the most sensitive area of Internet marketing. Although multiple messages may seem a good way of blanket covering your target audience, you must only do this if people have 'opted in' to receive such messages in the first place (either at your site or somewhere else).

The other problem with spam is that, because it is the preferred marketing method of illegitimate Internet companies, if you are seen to be spamming you risk being tarred with the same brush. Furthermore, Forrester Research estimates that by 2005 people will be burdened with over 50 e-mail messages a day. This means spamming is going to be deemed even more unwelcome in the near future.

Perhaps the strongest argument against spam, however, is that it doesn't work. It doesn't matter how many people you are targeting, if they haven't asked to receive messages from you and if they are not key members of your target audience, they aren't even going to open the message. They will simply click on the 'Delete' button in their e-mail program and block any further messages. If they remember the message at all, it will be in a negative rather than positive light. Indeed, research seems to suggest that e-marketers have woken up to this fact and are increasingly only sending messages to 'opt in' lists. According to Forrester Research, 77 per cent of companies that use e-mail marketing methods only send to customers who have asked for it. However, as we shall see towards the end of this chapter, there are instances when unsolicited e-mails can receive a positive response.

For further information on what does and does not constitute spamming, have a look at the following online resources:

Junkbusters (www.junkbusters.com)
StopSpam (stopspam.oreilly.com)
The Coalition Against Unsolicited Commercial E-mail (www.cauce.org)
Spam Abuse (spam.abuse.net)

Incidentally, in case you were wondering, the term 'spam' comes from Monty Python's 'Spam, Spam, Spam' sketch in which spam is served with everything.

Privacy issues

Related to spam is the issue of privacy. As the Internet has developed, legislators have grown increasingly concerned about the way personal information can be used and misused by companies and individuals on the Internet. In the UK, partly as a response to this mounting concern, the Data Protection Act was passed, which means that, by and large, companies need to get permission from the individuals concerned before sending bulk e-mails to customers.

Attachments

Attachments are best avoided when sending out e-mails to your target audience. First, many people are worried about opening attachments for fear of infecting their computer system with a virus. If you send all the message in a plain text e-mail format, on the other hand, there is no risk of viruses. Secondly, opening an attachment requires two actions on the part of the recipient. Not only do they have to decide whether to click on the e-mail message itself but then they also have to make the decision as to whether to open the attached file. After all, nothing is more annoying on the Internet than waiting for a large attachment to download, opening it up and then discovering that it is irrelevant to you and therefore a waste of time.

Another reason not to send attachments during your direct e-marketing campaigns is that often recipients are unable to open them for one reason or another.

Formatting

Although sending messages using a plain text format may seem a boring option, it is often the most reliable. The reason for this is that although you may be able to create HTML formatted messages via e-mail, your recipient's e-mail system may not be able to support them. You should therefore check before you send an HTML formatted message or newsletter that the recipients will be able to read it on their e-mail software.

E-mailing lists

The easiest way to compile an e-mailing list is to provide people with an incentive to give you their e-mail addresses. This could be an automatic entry to a competition you are running or a free subscription to your online newsletter. Of course, there are many other ways to collect e-mail addresses. You could, for instance, make part of your site only accessible to people who type in a password and their e-mail address. You could even buy a list of e-mail addresses from a marketing firm which specializes in that area.

The problem with both of these options is that the e-mail addresses you collect will not be from people who have requested information from you. As we have seen elsewhere, the key to e-marketing success lies partly in getting people to pull material towards them. If you are sending e-mails to people who have not explicitly 'opted in' to your e-mailing list, or to people who have no interest in what you have to say, then you will be greeted with considerable disdain. Therefore, to create an e-mailing list that will prove itself of real value to your online marketing efforts, you will need to let people know why you want their e-mail address as well as why they should give it to you.

Subscribers should also be told before they opt in how they can unsubscribe. Here's an example of a subscriber message that can be placed on a Web site:

> To subscribe to The Chocoholic List send an e-mail to list@chocoholic.com with a blank subject line and the message 'subscribe chocoholic'. To unsubscribe change the message to 'unsubscribe chocoholic'.

Although you can create a passive mailing list by simply storing e-mail addresses in a word processing file, if you want to create an active list (in which subscribers can post messages to each other) you will need to use a special program such as Listserve (www.listserve.com) or Majordomo (www.majordomo.com) (see mailing list options, below).

While active lists give you less control they can prove more effective in building long-term relationships and enable you to engage in a mutually beneficial conversation with your subscribers. Active lists not only let recipients respond to messages, but they also let everyone else on the list see their responses. However, this can be a mixed blessing. The effort and commitment required in managing and editing an active list can be considerable. Of course, it is possible to create an unmoderated active list, but without moderation lists have a tendency to lose focus.

Mailing list options

Once you have decided to create an e-mailing list, you then need to consider *how* you are going to create and manage it. There are three basic options. You can either use your e-mail program to store all the addresses, use a free Web-based service, or use a fee-based MLM (Mailing List Management) service. Your decision will depend on various factors specific to your own e-marketing efforts. These factors will include the anticipated size of your mailing list, the time you can devote to it, your direct marketing budget and the specific way you want your list to operate. Below is a brief overview of each of these options.

Managing a mailing list on your e-mail program

The simplest way to organize your own mailing list is to store all the e-mail addresses in your software program. This involves placing an entry on your e-mail 'address book' (all the major e-mail software programs offer this facility) with the name of the mailing list you want to create (for instance 'Newsletter'), and then store all the subscriber addresses in that entry. Then when you want to send out your newsletter or other promotional material to this particular mailing list, simply address the posting to the relevant address book entry.

Although this method works best for *passive* mailing lists, it is possible to engage in some form of two-way interactivity. When your mailing list subscribers want to send a message to the list they can send the message to you, for it to be forwarded to other subscribers. To move even closer towards a two-way, *active* list you could use an e-mail software program that can automatically forward messages sent by each subscriber. For instance, the Eudora Pro software program enables you to create a filter that automatically forwards messages sent to you, provided they contain a specific keyword in the subject line of the message. By setting Eudora to check your inbox on a regular basis, mailing list messages can be distributed within a short timeframe and with no effort required from you. For information on how to create filters in your e-mail program visit the list manager's manual at List Proc (www.cren.net/listproc).

Using a free web-based mailing list service

There are various services on the Web that can manage your mailing list for free. However, in return for this free service you are obliged to display ads at the end of any message you distribute using the service. Furthermore, depending on the service, you may be afforded little control over which ads appear. Two of the most popular free Web-based mailing list services available are eGroups (www.egroups.com), and List One (www.listone.com)

One useful service that will help you manage your list is Listbot (www.listbot.com). The service offers free mailing list management and enables you to archive the messages you send and also find out demographic information about your subscribers. Furthermore, if you are compiling a mailing list from your Web site, Listbot will be able to manage your list without you having to download software. The best thing about Listbot, however, is that it allows you to divide the list into different sections, so that you can create lots of 'mini-lists' relating to specific areas. As with the other two services the reason the service is free is because the messages you send to people will include small ads placed by Listbot.

Fee-based mailing list management programs

If you want to use a program that handles subscription requests on your behalf and distributes messages instantaneously and automatically, you will have to pay for the privilege. The three main programs are Listserve (www.listserve.com), List Proc (www.listproc.net) and Majordomo (www.majordomo.com). The MLM programs enable you to specify whether you want a moderated or unmoderated, active or passive list. Once you have done this you will then need to send a welcome message to the MLM program, for automatic distribution when people subscribe to the list. This message should include instructions on how subscribers can use the list. To manage the list you will need to send specific commands to the MLM address you are given.

These commands enable the program to add and delete subscribers and (if you have an active list) to approve and reject messages posted by subscribers. These commands vary according to the specific program.

Whichever mailing list option you choose, you should consider promoting the list beyond your Web site. If the list is open for anyone to subscribe to, visit the Liszt Web site (www.liszt.com) and follow the steps to have your list added to its index and search engine. As well as Liszt you could promote (as tactfully as possible) your list newsletter in newsgroups and even in other mailing list discussion groups.

Writing for e-mail

Whether you are sending an e-mailout to your entire mailing list, or simply responding to an enquiry, it is important that you understand how effective e-mails are put together. Moreover, although e-mail is arguably the most revolutionary communication tool ever invented, it is not an end in itself. Just because you can send an e-mail doesn't necessarily mean your message is getting heard. As Edward de Bono observes in his book *New Thinking for the New Millennium*, 'the ability to send hundreds of e-mails does not ensure the ability to write something intelligent or amusing'.

The most important thing to remember when writing e-mails, is to write in your natural voice. Many of the formalities of letter writing should be discarded when you are approaching prospects via e-mail. Formal salutations such as 'Dear Mr Humphries', 'Dear Sir/Madam' and 'Dear Frances' are inappropriate, even when contacting someone for the first time. Similarly, there is no need for a 'Yours Sincerely' or a 'Yours Faithfully' at the foot of a message. Whereas a letter may end with a sentence such as: 'Should you require any further information please do not hesitate to contact me', it is much better to close an e-mail with the more informal, 'Please contact me if you have any questions.'

You also need to remember that people don't have time to read an e-mail message twice. When you send them a message about your company it will probably arrive in a mailbox with around five or six other unread messages. Your messages must be instantly accessible and easy for anyone to understand. Furthermore, e-mail is a tool of conversation. It is used by people to communicate with friends on a daily basis. Messages are sent and responded to in a matter of hours. As a result, e-mail messages are shorter and more conversational than most other forms of written communication. To use e-mail effectively as a direct marketing tool, it is therefore helpful to see it as a means of initiating a conversation.

Here are some ways to turn a sales pitch into the start of a mutually rewarding conversation.

Use humour

Many people believe humour is inappropriate for any business communication, either online or offline. They say 'It's personal' or, 'What might seem funny to you might not be funny to someone else.' But it is precisely the personal nature of humour that makes it appropriate for e-mail. If you can make someone smile or laugh you have made a connection on which you can build. This doesn't mean you have to go over the top, it just means you should try and speak in your 'authentic voice'. As Doc Searls writes on the Cluetrain Web site, 'Humour is, in most cases, a prerequisite for personal authenticity . If you're not laughing at yourself, are you really being honest about yourself? ... Your company can't engage in the market conversation without its authentic voice.' Humour is especially useful when you are contacting someone for the first time as it can make people warm to your message.

Ask questions

Asking questions is one of the easiest ways to keep a conversation alive, and can therefore improve your chances of winning the recipient's favour. Furthermore, questions indicate that you are a business that is ready and willing to listen to the voice of its customers (both actual and potential). These questions can relate to your business such as: 'Have you any useful ideas for people we could invite to answer questions in our discussion group?' or, 'Are there any services/products you would like to see us provide?'

If you ask open questions you are also likely to learn more about the people you are sending to, and this will enable you to personalize future messages to a greater extent. In theory at least, you can ask your individual customers exactly what they want from you, and then provide them with a situation that fits them perfectly.

Write in plain language

Both the official business writing style and advertising jargon must be equally resisted. E-mail is a much more immediate medium than paper and should be treated as such. People write and read messages at a completely different pace to writing a letter. The writing style you adopt should therefore not only be succinct and to the point, but also written in plain English.

Cyberspeak

Due to the immediate and informal nature of e-mail and discussion groups, various symbols and acronyms are used as a form of familiar shorthand. While it may not always be suitable to incorporate 'cyberspeak' into your e-mail correspondence, peppering your newsgroup messages with the odd 'emoticon' (short for emotional icon) will increase your status as a committed net head. Furthermore, when you are lurking in a Usenet newsgroup to get the feel for what type of message would be suitable to post, an understanding of net language will go a long way.

In 1999, it seemed like cyberspeak was all but a relic of the Internet's Dark Ages when it was the preserve of technologically minded students and researchers. Recently, however, the growing popularity of the mobile Internet, chat rooms, newsgroups and e-mail in general means that more and more people are familiar with the following examples of cyberspeak.

Emoticons

Because e-mail and newsgroup messages are written it can be difficult to detect the tone of a message, so emoticons (often referred to as 'smileys') are used to convey emotion in e-mail and newsgroup messages. Most emoticons are intended to represent a face on its side (tilt your head to the left to see each face) while others are a bit more abstract. While the following emoticons shouldn't be used in a business-to-business newsletter, they are widely accepted (indeed encouraged) in a lot of newsgroup discussions and can also be used effectively when targeting the youth consumer market:

:-)	Smiling (a happy face)
;-)	A wink
:-D	Laughing
:-(	Upset (an unhappy face)
8-)	Cool (a happy face wearing sunglasses)
:- /	Bemusement (a puzzled face)
X=	Fingers crossed
$-)	Greedy
X-)	I see nothing.

Acronyms

Acronyms are even more widely used than emoticons and they are a regular occurrence in e-mail messages as well as discussion groups. LOL (laughing out loud), BFN (Bye for now) and IMHO (in my humble opinion) in particular, are used frequently in e-mail messages. Here are some more to watch out for:

AFK	Away from Keyboard
BAK	Back at keyboard
BBL	Be back later
BD	Big deal
BFN	Bye for now
BRB	Be right back
BTW	By the way
CU	See you
FB	Furrowed brow
GAL	Get a Life
GR8	Great
GTRM	Going to read e-mail
HTH	Hope this helps
IMHO	In my humble opinion
IYSWIM	If you see what I mean
IAE	In any event
IOW	In other words
LOL	Laughing out loud
NRN	No reply necessary
OIC	Oh I see
OTOH	On the other hand
PBT	Pay Back Time
ROFL	Roll on the floor laughing
RTM or RTFM	Read the manual
SOL	Sooner or later
TIA	Thanks in advance
TTYL	Talk to you later
YL/YM	Young lady/Young man

Emphasis

One of the problems with e-mail is that italicized and bold lettering often cannot be interpreted by the recipient's software program. As a result many e-mail users have taken to enclosing words within asterisks, like *this*.

E-newsletters

Electronic newsletters can be an excellent direct marketing tool, as they enable you to communicate with your audience directly but also at a deeper level than a standard e-mail message. Of course, it can be argued that traditional *offline* newsletters can equally be used to build relationships at a deeper level than other traditional direct marketing methods. There are, however, a number of reasons why sending an e-newsletter is more effective than sending out a printed newsletter via the postal service. For a start, the considerable printing and postage costs involved in distributing newsletters offline are avoided altogether online. Furthermore, e-newsletters can be made interactive through links and can therefore *involve* the reader to a greater extent than they could offline; this means you can use them to build two-way, as opposed to one-way relationships. Another argument in favour of e-newsletters is that although they require you to invest a considerable amount of time in putting them together, they can be distributed simultaneously to thousands of people in an instant.

The main reason e-newsletters can be effective is because they combine 'push' and 'pull' marketing techniques. As we have discussed elsewhere, push marketing is where information is pushed towards the recipient, whereas pull marketing depends on people pulling information towards them. As an e-newsletter is sent out directly to people's e-mail boxes it can be considered a push technique, but in another sense recipients have pulled the newsletter towards them by subscribing to it.

As a result of this push-pull combination e-newsletters can be used to:

- *Build brand awareness.* Distributing e-newsletters on a regular basis will help build brand awareness by not only reminding people you still exist, but also by letting them know what you stand for.
- *Generate repeat traffic.* Attracting a link to your site and including extracted articles from your site are two tried and tested ways of using online newsletters to encourage repeat site traffic.
- *Enhance your authority status.* By providing informative and objective articles of interest to clients, customers and even competitors you can enhance your reputation as an authority on your business area.

- *Increase a customer's 'lifetime value'.* By subscribing to a newsletter visitors are, in effect, volunteering to engage in some form of long-term relationship with your business.
- *Compile a mailing list.* Newsletters provide the ultimate incentive for visitors to give you their e-mail addresses.
- *Conduct customer research.* E-mail or HTML formatted surveys can be incorporated within newsletters in order for you to conduct customer research.

Putting together material for your newsletter

The reason most people go online is to find answers to questions and solutions to problems, whether they look for these via the Web, discussion groups or e-mail. If people subscribe to an e-newsletter they therefore want information, not to read your catch line and mission statement over and over again.

Successful newsletters are about your audience, not your company. Of course, you should write about your company but only where it is of direct interest to people who buy your products. If you are in the service sector the content could follow a guide format, offering free advice to establish your expertise.

E-marketing success is, as we have discovered, dependent on the willingness and ability to provide useful and relevant information. Here are some guidelines to follow when turning your newsletter into an informative and valued resource:

- Encourage contributions from subscribers.
- Include links to other relevant sites and Web pages.
- Incorporate content from your site.
- Include a question and answer page.

Building trust with your e-newsletter

Successful relationships with your audience are based on the following two things: providing something people will find useful and establishing trust. To do both of these with your e-newsletter you need to make it as objective as possible.

Blatant self-promotion will be counter-productive in your e-newsletter. In line with the law of diminishing returns, the more your company, product or service name is referred to, the more authority over your audience you lose. While you must make sure recipients are fully aware that the newsletter is your business publication, you need to limit any blatant bias towards your company.

Here are some ways to increase the value of your newsletter by rendering it more objective:

- Send out an e-mail to relevant journalists asking if they would be willing to write an article for your newsletter. (If you can afford to pay for the privilege, there should be no problem.)
- Stick to material relevant to your business area, as opposed to your business interest.
- Gather feedback from subscribers via e-mail and incorporate some of the comments into the newsletter.
- Ask to incorporate material from other sources: magazines; e-zines; web sites; other newsletters and so on.
- Include a question and answer page. Getting subscribers to e-mail questions provides you with a legitimate excuse to promote your business or Web site.

Another way to add authority to your online newsletter is to convert it into an e-zine. Although there is some overlap in the definitions of online newsletters and e-zines, there are some identifiable differences. Typically, for instance, an e-zine is longer with a minimum of, say, 20 pages. Also, e-zines are often Web-based and are therefore written in HTML code script and are often available at a URL (Web site address) as well as via e-mail.

E-zines can be a worthwhile alternative to an online newsletter as they can provide your audiences with a glossier and lengthier source of information. However, e-zines will cost you more in terms of time, money and resources than an online newsletter. Furthermore, e-zines are distributed via HTML mail (e-mail messages that are formatted using HTML coding), which is incompatible with some e-mail programs. Unless you are absolutely certain every subscriber has an e-mail program that can translate HTML, you should stick to a plain text newsletter.

Length and frequency

There is no hard and fast rule as to how long your online newsletter should be. Indeed less can often prove to be more. One or two articles, a question and answer page, and a brief 'Note from the Editor', together totalling between 1000 and 2000 words may prove to be enough. After all, you do not want to frighten off your subscribers by burdening them with too much information. The danger with really long newsletters is that, regardless of how useful they are, they have a tendency to get deleted before they are read. Then again, if you have a loyal readership, a longer newsletter may prove more worthwhile as people may want to print it. For instance, Wilson Web's *Web Marketing* now has over 100,000 subscribers even though it weighs in at around 10,000 words. Clearly in this case, people are prepared to print out the newsletter because they really value its content. If you are unsure about the most suitable length for your newsletter, you could e-mail some of your subscribers to ask their opinion.

The length of your newsletter will probably affect its frequency. After all, lengthy newsletters take time to produce. If numerous people share publishing duties then obviously you can send out a newsletter more often than if you were compiling it single-handed. However, if a newsletter is sent out on a daily or even weekly basis recipients may end up unsubscribing simply because they don't have time to read it. Most successful newsletters, of whatever length, are sent out on a fortnightly or a monthly basis.

Formatting your e-newsletter

No matter how impressive the content of your newsletter is, there is little point sending it out if people are unable to read it because it has been formatted incorrectly. Here are some guidelines to ensure it can be read using a variety of e-mail software:

- Don't centre your text. As the newsletter will appear differently on different e-mail programs, don't try and centre or justify your text as it may look drastically different on someone else's computer screen.
- Keep columns under 70 characters long.
- Place spaces between paragraphs to make the text easier to read.
- Avoid monospace fonts such as Ariel and Courier, in which every letter takes up the same amount of space. The fonts look entirely different on each e-mail software program. When in doubt, Times Roman is always a safe option.
- Remember to spell check your newsletter.

- Before you send out your newsletter, send a copy to yourself or a colleague to check that it looks alright.
- Make sure you include the http:// part of any Web site address you mention as most e-mail programs will then be able to automatically convert the text into a link.

Distributing your e-newsletter

When it comes to distributing a newsletter online you have two basic options: do it yourself or pay a company to do it for you. Distributing a newsletter yourself has obvious advantages. As well as saving money you have complete control over when your newsletter is issued and to whom.

Having said that, distributing a newsletter takes a lot of time, particularly when you have a large subscriber base. Furthermore, if you have over 1000 subscribers, you are letting yourself in for a complicated administrative task. The mere act of adding and removing subscribers becomes a considerable chore. It is no surprise, then, that many companies with substantial marketing budgets opt to outsource the distribution (and, in many cases, the compilation) of their newsletter to e-mail marketing companies. According to Forrester Research, the market for these types of services will reach $4.8 billion a year by 2004, up from $156 million in 1999, when Forrester started the research. However, although e-mail marketing companies such as FloNetwork (www.flonetwork.com) and Cheetah Mail (www.cheetahmail.com) are increasingly popular, their prices put them out of reach for the small or medium-sized business.

To distribute an online newsletter yourself you need to create your own subscriber list of e-mail addresses. For this you require a software program, such as Pegasus (http://www.pmail.com/) that can filter addresses in and out of the address book. Other major e-mail programs like Eudora Pro 4.1 and Outlook 2000 are unable to do this.

To collect e-mail addresses from your Web site you need to set up a subscription form that links to your e-mail system. The easiest way to so this is by using a Web building tool such as Adobe Page Mill, Microsoft Front Page or Dreamweaver, which will convert the HTML for you. However, when you first set up your newsletter you may find it easier still to get people to e-mail their contact details to you.

Posting your online newsletter

Once you have compiled your e-mail list you will then be able to send to multiple e-mail addresses simultaneously.

The way to do this properly involves using the Bcc: line. If you enter all the addresses into the To: or Cc: text boxes each recipient of the newsletter will be able to see the e-mail address of every other recipient. By using the Bcc: box you will be able to preserve the confidentiality of your subscription list, and avoid frustrating your subscribers by sending them a page full of e-mail addresses.

However, some programs will not allow you to use the Bcc: box alone as they will not send a message without an address in the To: line as well. The best thing to do in this case is to put your own address in the To: text box and send a copy of the newsletter to yourself.

Winning over potential subscribers

The best and most obvious place to promote your newsletter is on your Web site, as people will be able to sign up there and then. Whether you opt for a subscription form or simply ask people to e-mail their information to you, make sure you make it clear that any information people give you will remain confidential and will not be sold on to mailing list companies. Other ways to win over potential new subscribers include:

- Minimize the information you need. People are often put off when faced with lengthy forms to fill in.
- Make it easy for people to unsubscribe by providing an 'unsubscribe' option on your form, or by telling people they can unsubscribe by sending you an e-mail saying 'I want to unsubscribe'.
- Give details of the next issue date and indicate the frequency of the newsletter.
- Archive newsletters at your site.
- Submit your newsletter to those search engines that specifically cater for newsletters and e-zines such as E-Zinez (www.e-zinez.com), InfoBot (www.infobot.net) and Liszt (www.liszt.com).
- Provide a sample extract from the current newsletter on the subscription page.

- Indicate who the newsletter is aimed at and will appeal to as well as who has helped put it together. It is a good idea to allow at least two months for people to subscribe before the first issue date, so you can build up a substantial list of e-mail addresses.
- Encourage subscribers to pass the newsletter on to other people by including an 'e-mail this newsletter to a friend' option.

Although newsletters take time to produce, they can be a lot more effective than other forms of e-mail. As Simon Collin from Working Site (www.workingsite.com) confirms, 'If you want to create a hit-list of potential sales prospects, use e-mail lists and mail shots, but if you are in it for the long term then a regular newsletter is a great technique.' Furthermore, as e-marketing success now tends to be measured in terms of customers' 'lifetime value', newsletters are increasingly used as a means of building an ongoing sense of loyalty to a Web site.

Newsgroups

Newsgroups provide an online forum, collectively referred to as Usenet. Usenet's thousands of discussion forums provide an arena in which people can say almost anything relating to the forum's specific subject areas. Although they are similar to mailing lists, newsgroups collect messages on 'news servers' rather than via e-mail. As with mailing list discussion groups, newsgroups can be either moderated or unmoderated.

Newsgroups also differ from active mailing lists in the following respects:

- Visitors can follow the thread of a discussion group as messages are grouped with replies linked to the initial article.
- You can access a newsgroup using your Web browser.
- Most major search engines index newsgroup contents.
- Anyone can join a newsgroup.

Participation in these groups can be an extremely effective way of promoting your business. To succeed, however, you need to be able to promote your expertise rather than blatantly flaunt your products or services. Your success in a newsgroup is directly proportional to the amount of useful information you can offer. It goes almost without saying that if you provide people with useful answers to their questions, they will be receptive to learning more about your products or services.

The first step is to find newsgroups and mailing lists that will be useful to your business. The main searchable index of the Usenet groups can be found at Deja News (www.dejanews.com). However, you can also search through newsgroups at Yahoo! (dir.yahoo.com/Computers_and_Internet/Internet/Chats_and_ Forums/Usenet/Newsgroups_Directories/). After entering key-words relevant to your business into the search engines, you'll get back a list of messages that contain those keywords, along with the names of the discussion groups where they appear most frequently. This gives you a good indication of the groups that will be most receptive to your direct marketing effort. Read the descrip-tion of the group and its code of conduct to see if new site announcements are welcomed or if the group is restricted to the realm of non-commercial discussion.

To use newsgroups effectively, you should follow the guidelines outlined below.

Lurk

Before you start posting messages to discussion groups you should *lurk* for a while by reading the messages without taking an active part in the group. This will enable you to appreciate the way members of the group interact with each other, and you will get an idea of the sort of messages that will go down well and get the biggest response. You will also be able to make sure that the discus-sion group is appropriate for your purposes and that your mes-sages will reach a relevant and considerable target audience.

To promote your business or site in discussion groups takes con-siderable time and care. One of the biggest mistakes a business can make is to rush headlong into a group directly promoting its site and services without understanding the needs and interests of the group contributors. You will need to read a lot of postings – many lists generate hundreds of messages every day – to check for mes-sages that ask questions that enable you to show off your expertise.

Create a 'signature line'

A good 'signature line' is needed before you start posting to dis-cussion groups. A signature line is a sentence at the end of your message that says something about you, your business or your site.

The signature line offers space for the sort of direct self-promotion that is unavailable in the message above it. Provided the message is intelligent and useful, your signature line will be great promotion for your business.

Signature lines are the acceptable face of free advertising on the web. To my best knowledge, no one has ever been rebuked or 'flamed' for information about their Web site that they have included in their signature line.

It should be remembered, however, that the main purpose of a signature line is to provide contact information. Advertising your site must be seen as secondary. Typically a signature line should consist of your name, position, Web address, e-mail address, other contact details as well as information on the latest developments on your site and any forthcoming online events.

Contextualize your messages

Newsgroups and mailing lists are established on the basis of a shared interest – be that accountancy, feng shui or horse riding. Therefore, when you participate in a discussion make sure your message is relevant to the context. Don't try and sell your financial services in a group for booklovers. However, it is not just the topic of your messages that need to be in context, but also the tone.

Members of newsgroups generally want advice, not advertising. If you do want to use newsgroups in a blatantly commercial manner, there are newsgroups especially assigned for this purpose. In a normal newsgroup, leave the advertising for your signature line and stick with providing helpful information or advice in the body of the message.

The easiest way to place your message in context is to quote from the message you are responding to. That way you will look like you are participating in an existing discussion rather than starting a new one of your own.

Don't post too many messages

Only post occasionally when you have something of value to offer. Perhaps even more importantly, never post the same message to more than one group, as readers of one group are likely to read others.

Become a system operator

If you want to have even greater influence within a newsgroup you can apply to become part of the group's administration as a system operator. If you think of a topic you know well that will have an ongoing appeal on a relevant message board, post your suggestion to the moderator of the newsgroup. This is a particularly good idea if you are a consultant or adviser, as it will allow you to demonstrate your expertise from a position of authority.

Answer questions

The quickest way to build up credibility in newsgroups is to provide useful answers to questions. Even if the question doesn't directly relate to your business, if you can answer it, do so. People will not only see your business information in your signature line, but also you will be appreciated for providing something for free. Furthermore, you will build up your reputation as a good 'netizen' (online citizen) and be in a better position to promote your business when the right opportunity arises.

If you cannot find any relevant questions that would allow you to show off your expertise, it is still possible to contribute by posting an advice article, such as 'Ten Top Tips' on something, or by asking a question that will help you conduct market research.

Although participating in newsgroups can be one of the most effective ways of communicating your business message to new audiences, a great deal of sensitivity is needed to build up trust in these groups. Many business people use these groups so indiscriminately that they give the group, as well as their business, a bad name. If you push your business too hard in a newsgroup or mailing list, you suffer the humiliation of being *flamed*. That is to say you will receive protests from all the other members who do not appreciate such direct promotional tactics. Many people have used them to great effect, particularly to promote themselves as specialists in their business area. This form of direct marketing takes time and patience to carry out successfully, but it is ultimately one of the most cost-effective means of generating an online buzz about your company or Web site.

A brief guide to netiquette

The fact that e-mail is a relatively informal medium does not mean anything goes. The unintentional abuse of e-mail by many companies can seriously damage their healthy reputation. In fact, according to a survey carried out by InTuition, 58 per cent of companies believe e-mail messages can 'cause misunderstanding and damage relationships'.

Netiquette, or online etiquette, therefore must be adhered to by e-marketers when contacting customers and prospects via e-mail (or in discussion groups). By abiding by the following guidelines, you can increase your chances of a positive response:

- *Be obvious*. Always make it obvious why you are sending the message. Also, make sure that each e-mail or discussion group article you post has a definite and obvious purpose.
- *Be polite*. Even if you are responding to a hostile message in a discussion group, always maintain a polite tone.
- *Be legal*. Ensure that you protect any legally sensitive information and use disclaimer notices where necessary.
- *Use type cases appropriately*. Many e-marketers seem to believe using uppercase letters makes more of an impact. In fact, writing in capital letters puts people off, as it makes the message look like spam. Equally, text written entirely in lower case can give the impression that it was put together in a hurry or that the author couldn't be bothered.
- *Avoid vague subject lines*. Subject lines for e-mail and discussion group messages must be self-explanatory. Vague subject lines, such as 'Information' or 'About your phone call', must be avoided in favour of meaningful and relevant subject lines.
- *Reveal identities*. Make sure (especially in discussion groups) that people are aware who is sending the message.
- *Be honest*. If you are sending a commercial message, be upfront and honest about the fact.
- *Don't spam*. Internet Service Providers and recipients view unsolicited and indiscriminate mass mailings with disdain.
- *Check the address*. Messages that end up in the wrong mailboxes do little for your company's reputation.
- *Avoid attachments*. As mentioned earlier in this chapter, people are often hesitant about opening attached files for fear of computer viruses.
- *Provide an 'unsubscribe' option*. Messages sent via your e-mailing list must always make clear how the recipient can opt out or unsubscribe.
- *Respect privacy*. If you are collecting e-mail addresses, be explicit about the fact that you will not sell on e-mail addresses to other companies.

Case study: MP3.com (www.MP3.com)

MP3.com, the Internet music service provider that enables people to download music files from each other's computers, has always incorporated direct e-mail marketing techniques within its promotional strategy. The most radical use of e-mail occurred when the service introduced a new method for releasing singles by e-mailing digital files of tracks to its hundreds of thousands of opt-in subscribers.

The technique was first initiated in Autumn 2000 when MP3.com joined forces with the Warner Music Group. According to MP3.com's chairman and CEO, Michael Robertson, the service 'gives major record labels the opportunity to achieve full media saturation immediately upon the release of new music'.

The e-mails incorporate a link to the recording artist or record label's Web site, 'a forward-to-a-friend' link as well as radio and MTV request links (see Figure 7.1). More significantly, each e-mail includes a 'buy' link that connects to an online retailer where the user can purchase music immediately. Michael Robertson

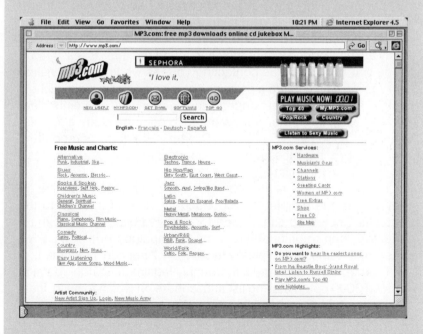

Figure 7.1 MP3 Web site. MP3.com pioneered 'singleserving' via e-mail

claims that this technique, which capitalizes on MP3.com's revolutionary technology and vast database, is set to 'give record labels a remarkable complement to their traditional promotional and marketing efforts'.

Case study: Thomas Cook (www.thomascook.com)

Thomas Cook is one company that has shown that 'friendly spam' can work. The problem it faced was that although it had compiled a database of around 17,000 e-mail addresses, it hadn't received the green light to send electronic mailshots to each address. As the database was being compiled, Thomas Cook had no idea as to how it would eventually use the addresses, so it hadn't thought to ask the people who provided their e-mail addresses whether or not they would mind being contacted by Thomas Cook in the future.

The company was anxious not to offend its customers by sending inappropriate spam messages, but also didn't want to simply throw away the e-mail addresses it had compiled. It therefore planned an e-mail campaign that would be unlikely to cause much annoyance. The first e-mailshot it sent to the list immediately acknowledged where they had found the addresses; it ran: 'I hope you don't mind us contacting you, as we know you visited our site...'. It also made a promise not to send any more mailshots unless the recipient responded. Having made these points clear straightaway, the e-mail then went on to offer the chance to enter Thomas Cook's 'Win Your Dream Holiday' competition. Furthermore, the message was kept deliberately short, so that it wouldn't take much time or effort to read.

The result of this responsible and tactful approach was that 19 per cent of the recipients responded by clicking through to the Thomas Cook Web site. It therefore proved over 10 times more effective than traditional direct mail campaigns (the company's direct mail campaigns typically receive a 1.7 per cent response).

Thomas Cook now had a thoroughly legitimate starting point of around 3000 opt-in mailing list subscribers on which to build. It did this through its Summer 2000 'Free Weekend Breaks' promotion, whereby the chance of winning breaks was offered on the site to new customers as an incentive for people to opt-in to the Thomas

Cook e-mail list. This time, Thomas Cook wanted more information than just e-mail addresses so subscribers were asked to select their preferred destinations. To expand the growth of their opt-in list even more dramatically, visitors to the site could e-mail as many as nine friends to tell them about the Free Weekend Breaks offer.

Although the offer was intended to generate the ambitious total of around 100,000 within four weeks, the end result was far more impressive. Within the space of a fortnight the site had over 250,000 new opt-in subscribers.

Summary

To use the Internet to its full marketing potential, you need to think beyond Web sites. E-mail and newsgroups provide you with the means of taking your business message to your target audience, rather than having to wait for your target audience to come to you. As this chapter has shown, although direct marketing on the Internet needs to be conducted with particular care, if you take a responsible approach it can be the key to long-term online success.

eight

Handling sales
online

As we have already discovered, the Internet is a great way for businesses to promote themselves as it enables them to communicate their message directly to their target audience. However, if you only use the Internet as a *promotional* tool, you will be neglecting those members of your target audience who are willing to spend money online. If you sell products or services in the real world, customers will soon expect you to handle sales online as well. Furthermore, by converting your site from a promotional aid into a fully functional e-commerce operation you will be able to reach out to potential new customers around the world. This chapter looks at the practical issues involved in doing, rather than simply promoting, business on the Internet.

Selling on the Web

The first thing you need to appreciate is that some products transfer better to the Internet than others. As the success of Amazon and CDNow testify, books and music have traditionally fared well on the Web. One of the reasons is that customers don't need to see or touch these products to know if they want to buy them. They either want them or they don't, it's as simple as that.

Another reason these products do well online has to do with what e-marketers term the Internet's 'database functionality'. In other words, the Internet enables users to search through vast inventories within a matter of seconds. Furthermore, ordering a book or CD online is not too risky for the first-time e-shopper as the price is relatively low and delivery straightforward.

After music and books, it is computer hardware and software that customers are most willing to buy online. This can probably be attributed to the fact that, at the moment at least, people who buy computer products are likely to be among those most comfortable and confident with using the Internet: most people still access the Internet via their home or office PC.

Products such as clothes, furniture and food, where there is a desire to touch or test before deciding to buy, inevitably do less well. However, as more and more people are getting used to shopping on the Web, virtually every product category is feeling the benefit.

Although books, CDs and computer products are the undisputed Internet bestsellers it does not necessarily mean that they are the easiest products for a newly established Web site to sell. After all, if your brand is not well recognized customers will be more likely to visit Amazon, CDNow or Dell Computers. In fact, the smaller sites that do well on the net steer clear of these mass markets and concentrate on niche products and services. Sites such as Hot Hot Hot (www.hothothot.com), which sticks to selling very hot chilli sauces, do really well by offering products not widely available on the average high street, but which when placed in front of a global audience have quite a substantial market.

The e-commerce sites that do well on the Internet fall into two distinct and opposing categories. At one end of the scale you have companies such as Amazon, which succeed by diversifying and expanding into other mass-market product categories, while at the other you have companies that achieve their marketing objectives by tightening their online niche.

Having said this, it is possible to exploit a niche *within* a mass market. For instance, the software company Anaconda (www.anaconda.net; see Figure 8.1) sells the software products used by Amazon affiliates. As Anaconda is the only business that develops and sells this niche software, it does not have to compete with the likes of Microsoft or Adobe.

If you are selling services rather than products, you may need to think a bit harder about the sales process. Whether you are using your site to promote a service offline, or you are actually selling a service at your site, you will have to provide a real example of how effective your service is. Simply telling people is rarely enough. You may have to offer limited free advice, or some other proof of your service's value.

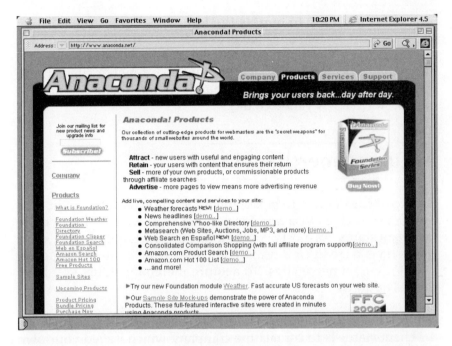

Figure 8.1 Anaconda Web site. Anaconda exploits a niche within an established market

Processing orders

As we have discussed elsewhere, HTML can be used to help you add forms to your site. However, while HTML is used to lay out your site and put the visual aspects of an order form together, it cannot make the form *work*. That is to say, while HTML allows you to design a box for people to submit their credit card details, it cannot actually process those details. For this you will need to set up what is commonly referred to as a 'shopping-cart system'. This enables order information to be calculated and sent back and forth between your Web server and the customer's Web browser.

There are three basic ways to add a shopping-cart system to your site: you can buy software, use a shopping-cart service, or set it up via your ISP. Many companies decide the latter option is the simplest, as ISPs (in most cases) will already have shopping-cart software installed on their server. They also tend to offer the most competitive rates. The other two options (buying software and using a shopping-cart service) are looked at in more depth below.

There is one way to bypass the issue of setting up your own shopping-cart system and that is to take part in an existing online shopping mall. There are a number of Web-based shopping malls out there offering 'floorspace' to new e-commerce sites. These include Barclay Square (www.barclaysquare.co.uk), and the Yahoo! store (www.yahoo.co.uk).

Acquiring merchant status

For credit card orders to be accepted and processed by credit card companies such as Visa and MasterCard, you will need to acquire merchant status. As most people buying products online will expect to do so via a credit card transaction, merchant status is absolutely vital for e-commerce sites. To acquire merchant status you have several options:

- *Your credit card company*. One of the easiest ways to receive merchant status is to contact the company which issued your own cards (either personal or business cards).
- *Your bank*. Merchant status can usually be acquired via your bank. If you are setting up an Internet-based company from scratch, this will probably involve going through your business plan with an account manager.
- *Your ISP*. Internet Service Providers often have partnerships with merchant account providers and can occasionally get you a better rate.
- *Your existing account holder*. If your business already operates in the real world, it generally makes sense to stick with the same merchant account holders.

When choosing your account you need to be aware that rates vary considerably. If you remain unsure, contact other e-commerce sites and ask how they made their decision over merchant status.

Shopping-cart software and services

There are various services and software products to help you set up an online shop. Here we take a look at two of the leading products,

Intershop and Click and Build, along with one of the most popular Web-based e-commerce services, Shop Site.

Intershop (www.intershop.com)

Intershop (see Figure 8.2) is a widely used e-commerce software product, targeted at businesses that are willing to offer template-based services to their clients. The Intershop product is available at three different levels of sophistication: ePages, Hosting and Merchant.

The highest level package, Merchant, can cater for just about any site, no matter how much traffic it receives. Furthermore, as well as incorporating a broad range of different templates that can be tagged on to an existing site, it can be used in conjunction with standard Web design products (such as Front Page or Dreamweaver) to create more personalized and individual e-shop designs. If you

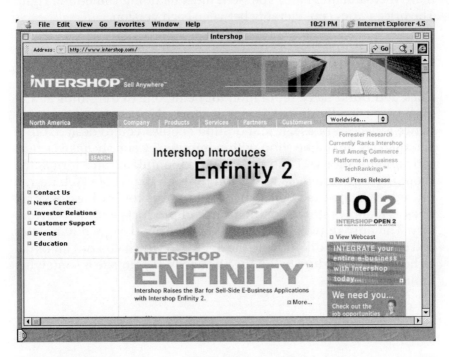

Figure 8.2 Intershop Web site. The Intershop product is available at three levels of sophistication

123

want your e-commerce site to show off a versatile range of multi-media elements, Merchant also lets you integrate audio, video and JavaScript (the Web-building code that enables dynamic and animated graphics to appear on a Web site). As well as enabling your site to process orders, it can also track customer accounts and control inventory. The Merchant package also offers various order, traffic and customer behaviour reports to help you understand your audience that little bit better. Intershop also covers your security concerns as all payment details are encrypted using a coding system called Secure Socket Layer (SSL) and each customer's details are encrypted and stored within the Intershop database. The other advantage of Intershop is that, at every level, it is easy to use, providing a simple point-and-click interface.

If you are running a small online operation, ePages is probably the best option, as many of the features incorporated within the Hosting and Merchant packages are unsuitable or irrelevant for smaller Web sites with a moderate flow of traffic. According to Dataquest, Intershop has a larger market share in e-commerce sales than Microsoft and Netscape, so it must be doing something right. The price varies considerably between each version.

Click and Build (www.clickandbuild.com)

Click and Build has a reputation for being one of the simplest and most user-friendly shop building products. No programming experience is necessary as Click and Build enables you to design, build and manage an online shop within minutes by simply answering a series of questions. Using pre-designed templates and forms, the shopping-cart system can take you through the whole Web design procedure if required. Click and Build caters for businesses of all sizes as it allows storage of thousands of products within its inventory. The only drawback is, as it relies on pre-designed templates and does all the work for you, the degree to which you can tailor the e-shopping procedure to the specific needs of your site is somewhat limited.

Shop Site (www.openmarket.com)

Shop Site is a shop building system aimed at the small to medium-sized business. Unlike Intershop, you do not have to install software onto your computer as it is a Web-based system run from the user-friendly Open Market site. Open Market takes you gently through the steps involved in setting up your own online shop. This includes filling in a few forms and choosing graphics to upload, but nothing too strenuous. The only drawback is that as you have to work with the design templates provided by Open Market, the visual design of your site can become slightly compromised. Having said that, it is possible to modify each template and edit individual pages, although this can be rather time-consuming.

Unlike other 'shop in a box' solutions, orders are not held on your Web server but on that of the Open Market site. When an order is processed an order notification message is sent to your e-mail address. As with all the other 'shop in a box' options, Shop Site supports credit card payments, although it can only handle two types of currency. As an *Internet* magazine reviewer concluded, 'overall this is a well-designed straightforward tool for building shop fronts that are functional but not too complex'.

Here is a selection of other e-commerce site building systems:

Catalog (www.actinic.co.uk)
Maestro Commerce (www.maestrocommerce.com)
Shop Zone Professional (www.btsw.com)
Verifone (www.verifone.com)
Web Sockets (www.websockets.com).

For more information on e-commerce software and services visit dir.yahoo.com / Business_and_Economy / Electronic_Commerce.

Whichever system you choose you should make sure it offers the following features:

- *A search option*. If you offer a wide range of products a search facility is essential.
- *Credit card verification*. You need to make sure that the system will confirm that credit card details, e-mail addresses and other personal details were entered in the correct format.
- *Automated e-mail*. Most systems enable you to send out an automated e-mail when a user has placed an order.
- *A shopping basket*. Internet shoppers have now come to expect a shopping basket facility on e-commerce sites. This enables them to add products to a basket, then to carry on shopping, adding more products as they go.

- *Continued shopping*. Many shopping-cart systems enable customers to leave the site, return, and continue shopping.
- *Flexible order options*. The system you choose should enable you to specify as many delivery and rate options as you require.
- *E-mail contact*. You will require a system that sends you a notification e-mail every time an order has been processed.
- *Instant transactions*. The best systems pass credit card details instantly to the card issuer to be accepted or declined there and then. This not only increases security but also prevents the customer frustration caused when an order is made and a credit card payment is declined a week later.
- *Multi-currency support*. If you plan to sell your products or services overseas, multi-currency support is essential (as are shipping rate and tax calculations).
- *Encryption*. Credit card details and other personal information entered by the user should be encrypted for maximum security.
- *Customization*. It is better to choose a system that enables you to adapt templates than one that offers minimal customization. Furthermore, you should choose a system that can be integrated with the rest of your site rather than one that forces you to take an 'all or nothing' approach.
- *Payment flexibility*. More sophisticated systems allow you to accept various forms of payment, and not just rely on the customers using Visa or MasterCard.
- *Order integration*. If you are a real world business embarking online you will need to ensure that the system you use enables your online shop to be integrated into your existing inventory and order systems.

Price pressure

In the real world companies generally set prices in relation to manufacturing, marketing and supply costs. On the Internet, however, the supply chain is reversed as the customer starts to wield all the power. The top-down pricing structure is replaced on the Web by a consumer-generated bottom-up model. There are many reasons why the Internet can cause downward pressure on prices. The first and most obvious has to do with comparative shopping. The huge variety of online retailers means it's easier for customers to compare prices. Internet users can visit similar businesses all around the world via the Internet in search of the cheapest products. Portal sites such as the BBC's Internet shopping service (www.beeb.com) make this even easier by providing instant price comparisons. There are also services such as Let's Buy It (www.letsbuyit.com) that lower prices by uniting customers together to buy products *en masse*. The more people use such services, the cheaper the products become.

Although this downward price pressure is undeniable, it does not mean you have to reduce your profit margins to zero. What it does mean, however, is that in order for you to keep prices at a level that suits you, it is necessary to integrate your product or service range with valuable and informative content.

Increasingly content is adding value to commerce and the opportunity to buy products is being used to make information more interactive. Here are several successful examples of the commerce/content overlap on the Web:

- *Advance Publications*. Advance Publications, the owner of the *Vogue* and *W* magazine titles, has set up an online magazine called Style.com (www.style.com). The site enables visitors not only to see and read about the latest fashions and style trends, but also to click on them and buy them through its own e-store.
- *ThinkNatural.com (www.thinknatural.com)*. Think Natural, the UK-based online health product retailer, supplies the information on MSN.com's women's channel.
- *BeingGirl.com (www.beinggirl.com)*. Being Girl is Procter and Gamble's site 'just for teens, with information on relationships, guys, periods and so much more'. As well as supplying frank information, it also promotes relevant Procter and Gamble brands such as Tampax, Always and Alldays.

As mentioned elsewhere in this book, affiliate marketing provides another way to mix content with commercial interests. On some affiliate sites, every time a book or other product is mentioned or reviewed, a neighbouring link connects with an ordering service that enables the visitor to purchase the item. The affiliate site then receives payment for either each click-through or sale to the site running the program.

Ultimately, online retailers must offer a lot of information about a product if they are to compensate both for the customers' inability to touch and feel each item and their ability to find the same products at cheaper prices elsewhere.

Auctioning products and services

One of the most effective ways of selling products or services from a Web site is to hold an online auction. Many companies have found very real advantages in auctioning their products and services and many marketers are now seeing auctions as more than just a one-off gimmick to increase visitor numbers. As a result, online auctions now constitute the fastest growing area of the whole e-commerce market. Here are some of the benefits an online auction could bring to your business:

- *Appropriate pricing*. Online auctions can help you discover the price your customers are willing to pay for new products or services.
- *More shoppers*. Auctions can help convert passive visitors into active e-shoppers because they intensify the buying environment.
- *Communal buying*. As any psychologist will tell you, behaviour breeds behaviour. Visitors are more likely to spend money on products if they can see other people doing the same.
- *Publicity*. Auctions add another media-friendly hook to get journalists interested in your site.
- *Interactivity*. Auctions add interaction to the buying process, not only between a customer and the site but also between a customer and other visitors.

The increased demand for Internet auctions has led to a variety of auction software products emerging on the market. Instil (www.instil.com) and Open Site (www.opensite.com) are two of the main companies satisfying the growing demand. Although prices and the degree of sophistication vary widely between software products, there are some common features inherent in most programs. These include keyword profiling to help organize products placed for auction, currency translators, and bulletin boards enabling vendor and purchaser feedback.

Most programs also take you through the auctioning process step by step. Typically, this involves:

- the site hosting the auction setting and publicizing auction schedules;

- potential bidders logging onto the auction site, registering and submitting their e-mail address and credit card details;
- products and services being bid for;
- once the auction is finished, the highest bidder being contacted by e-mail with all the relevant information.

Security issues

If you are taking customer details on your Web site or processing orders online you will need to use a 'secure server' system. Among other things, this enables credit card information typed into an order form to be encrypted before being sent from the customer's Web browser to the server. Although you don't have to have a secure server to take orders online, many users will be reluctant to purchase products via your Web site without one.

The predominant form of secure server is the SSL (Secure Socket Layer) server, which was first introduced by Netscape back in 1995. SSL is now recognized as *the* international standard for securing e-commerce activity. The encryption processes used by SSL technology are considered virtually impenetrable. Furthermore, regular e-shoppers have come to recognize the closed padlock or unbroken key symbol at the bottom of the 'checkout' page, which signifies that a site is using SSL. If the server is secure, users only need to take the same basic precautions as when they give credit card details over the phone. In fact, because no one at all gets to know the customer's card details, there is a strong argument to suggest that SSL-based credit card transactions are actually *more* secure than they are in the real world.

To implement secure server technology on your site you will need a Webserver certificate from Verisign (www.verisign.com) to prove you are a legal and trustworthy business (provided you are a legitimate business, the certificate is not very difficult to obtain). However, instead of seeking the certificate from Verisign yourself you will probably be able to use the certificate of your ISP or whoever is hosting your site. Your hosting service could deal with the whole process for you, although often for an additional fee.

However, simply having an SSL secure server is not enough, as you also need to make sure your customers feel safe. Below are some steps you can take to alleviate your site users' fears over e-commerce security.

Provide SSL information

Although many users recognize the SSL closed padlock or unbroken key symbol and are aware of what it signifies, many more do not. You should therefore tell people not only that you use a secure server, but also what that means exactly. As well as telling them how their credit card transaction is secured, you could also link to more detailed information on SSL and what it means for them.

Offer security advice

Internet users tend to prefer sites that are upfront about security issues to those that ignore their security concerns. By offering security advice you will also be able to put these concerns into context by telling users it is safer to place an order at a site using SSL technology than it is to pay for a meal at a restaurant.

Include a returns policy

Customers will be more likely to place trust in your site if they can see that you have a returns policy.

Replicate the real world shopping experience

One reason for the scepticism about e-commerce security is the fact that the Internet is still a relatively new medium. E-commerce sites that inject a sense of familiarity and references to the real world shopping experience can often alleviate fears over security.

'On the Internet, familiarity doesn't breed contempt', says Sophie Burke of Shoeworld.co.uk, 'it builds brand loyalty. With the use of recognizable icons, browsers are easily transposed from a traditional shopping experience to one that is online.' That's why most e-commerce sites have adopted the shopping basket analogy so that visitors can wander the online aisles, pick up what they want and then head for the checkout.

Publish a privacy policy

Publishing a privacy policy on your site, stating that personal details will remain secure, will help customers place their trust in your site.

A typical privacy policy would read as follows: 'As part of its guarantee, MySite.com promises never to sell, rent or trade personal information to a third party without your express permission.'

Provide assurances

Obviously it would be easy to tell people how secure your site is, but you will need to make any assurances credible. The best way to do this is to sign up to one of the growing number of online reassurance schemes intended to calm security fears. A good example is the Which? Webtrader Scheme (www.which.net/webtrader). To become a member, an e-commerce site must confirm that its shopping facilities are secure.

Other reassuring logos that can build customer trust include those of the Truste Scheme (www.truste.com) and the Clicksure Certified Merchant (www.clicksure.com). By getting in touch with these sites and taking part in their schemes, you can reassure your customers you're conforming to recognized Internet security standards.

Summary

Selling products and services online not only adds another revenue stream to your business, but it can also help build relationships with your target audience by turning passive visitors into active customers. To handle sales effectively you need to think very carefully about the type of shopping-cart system you can use, as well as other commerce issues such as security. To make sure your products or services sell, you will also need to think of ways to support customers before, during and after they make a purchase. This subject is explored in more detail in the next chapter.

nine

Supporting
customers

As Internet shopping is still a relatively new activity, effective customer support is essential if you are to convert browsers into buyers. To boost online sales you need to make the process of buying a product as easy as possible. The more work that is required on the part of the site visitor the less likely it is that a sale will be made, it's as simple as that. This chapter looks at the ways in which you can get customers to make that all-important first purchase, as well as to fulfil their expectations thereafter.

Winning over first-timers

Although Internet users on both sides of the Atlantic are now coming around to the idea of shopping online, it can still be an uphill struggle winning over e-shopper virgins. 'The hardest order is the first order', says Harry Ganz from the online pharmacy Garden (www.garden.co.uk). 'Give good service on the first order and you have a customer for life.'

This is an opinion supported elsewhere in the e-commerce community. For instance, Jim McFarlane from Pet Planet (www.petplanet.co.uk) also believes 'the issue is assuring first-time customers that we can be trusted. Once we deliver the first order without error or complication, the customer relaxes and starts to trust us'.

Therefore the question is, how can you convert someone who is happy to visit your site into someone who is happy to shop at your site? Here are some suggestions.

Alleviate security fears

As we discussed near the end of the previous chapter, your Web site not only needs to use an SSL server to ensure creditcard and transactions remain secure, but it also needs to make customers aware of what this actually means for them.

Don't oversell

If you look desperate to make a sale you will inevitably put people off. When people start to take their first tentative steps into the world of e-shopping they generally do so by making informed choices based on objective comment, rather than hyperbolic advertising.

Simplify the shopping process

Lengthy and complex e-shopping procedures are going to scare first-time customers away. Keep the shopping process as simple and convenient as possible. Make it easy for customers to be able to correct any errors of entry and ensure that the 'Back' button is all it takes to solve the problem. Take Amazon.com's legendary 'one-click shopping' system as your inspiration (don't follow it too closely, however, as they have patented it to prevent any copycat systems emerging). Avoid visual clutter on order forms and always tell users where they are in the ordering and registration process. You could also follow the lead of CDNow and provide confirmation to customers that they are doing the right things to accomplish a transaction.

Provide an FAQ page

Once your Web site has been up and running for a little while you will probably have received quite a few anxious enquiries from potential customers asking about various e-shopping issues. You could use these as the basis for an FAQ (Frequently Asked Questions) page on your site. This will help answer any concerns virgin visitors may have.

Typical questions seen on FAQ pages include: 'How long will I have to wait for my goods to be delivered?', 'How do I know that details I pass on to a Web site will not be disclosed to any third party?' and, 'What do I do if the goods are incorrect or faulty?' If you have the answers to these questions ready at hand you will be well on your way to winning over first-time customers.

Market researchers claim that the rate at which e-shoppers give up on the purchase they intend to make before reaching the online checkout is between 25 per cent (Andersen Consulting) and 78 per cent (Bizrate). Whichever report you choose to believe the difficulties e-tailers face in converting site visitors into site shoppers are very real. Every effort must therefore be made to provide first-timers with a hassle-free shopping environment.

Here are some sites that should inspire you in your quest to win over virgin shoppers:

- *Drugstore (www.drugstore.com).* Drugstore does not put off first-time visitors by hiding tax or shipping charges (see Figure 9.1). Instead, it presents all the additional costs before a customer reaches the order form.
- *Gap (www.gap.com).* The Gap Web site is quite rightly heralded as a supremely user-friendly shopping environment. One of the

Figure 9.1 The Drugstore Web site. Drugstore takes a decidedly upfront approach to pricing

reasons for this is that it lets customers put items to one side while they decide what to purchase. This enables customers to save items and return to purchase them later.

- *Jcrew (www.jcrew.com)*. Jcrew provides an excellent example of short and hassle-free order forms.
- *Toys R Us (www.toysrus.com)*. The Toys R Us site is widely regarded as one of the most customer-focused e-tail sites. Features include a customer service section, clear content listings, easy search facilities, help on how to order products, related links (to similar products within the site), availability information and visible shopping-cart contents.

Making subsequent sales

When customers buy a product from your site for the first time, they are doing so because they have a positive *expectation* of what and how you will deliver. To secure a second sale, however, customers must also have a positive *experience* of your site. In other words if you fail to fulfil customers' expectations on their first order they are unlikely to pay a return visit.

While the first sale is important, it is the second sale that really counts. This is because long-term cyberspace survival depends not on constantly seeking new customers but on building relationships with established ones. The buzz phrase in e-marketing circles is now 'lifetime value'. If you can increase each customer's 'lifetime value' by generating repeat sales, half the battle has been won.

The other reason you need to make sure that each customer's experience of your site's e-shopping procedure is a positive one has to do with the two-way nature of the Internet itself. Consumer feedback sites, Usenet newsgroups and e-mail-based discussion groups can all provide disgruntled customers with a means of expressing their discontent to entire online communities.

To increase your chances of repeat sales, you need to understand where many other Web sites go wrong. This view is also supported by none other than Jeff Bezos, chief executive and co-founder of Amazon.com, who recognizes that 'the thing that will kill Amazon and any other Internet company is bad customer experience'.

To make sure your customers are willing to return to your site and perhaps more importantly, are willing to spend more money at your site, you need to limit the potential for the 'bad customer experience' Bezos talks about. Here are 10 ways to add to the 'lifetime value' of your customers through successful fulfilment:

1. *Deliver on time.* Don't offer next-day delivery unless you can really provide that service. If, for any reason, a delivery is going to be late notify the customer via e-mail immediately.
2. *Check out your subcontractors.* One important lesson many e-commerce sites have had to learn is that if third parties are involved something can, and all too often will go wrong. Don't subcontract sales to companies that may not be able to meet set timescales. After all the customer has trusted your Web site, not a courier service.
3. *Have a tracking system.* Customers have the right to know where their goods are at any stage between order and delivery. Rather than wait for them to ask, take the initiative by e-mailing them when the product has been sent on its way to their doorstep.
4. *Reveal the full costs.* If you hide additional tax or postage costs you are unlikely to make a second sale.
5. *Make the availability of goods clear.* If customers are told at the last hurdle that a product is not available they will justifiably feel frustrated. As with pricing, it is better in the long term to be upfront and honest from the outset.
6. *Be prepared to refund goods.* If a customer is dissatisfied with a product it is better to provide a refund than to risk negative publicity online.
7. *Provide different delivery options.* You can personalize the delivery process by offering a range of different delivery times. Some customers will be prepared to pay more for shorter delivery times.
8. *Send goods out with receipts.* A surprisingly large number of e-commerce sites don't provide receipts, leaving customers with a bad impression of the site and its service.
9. *Offer live customer support.* Online vendors must offer live customer support, either via e-mail or phone, if they are to meet the expectations of their customers.
10. *Keep forms as short as possible.* Do not use order forms as market research tools. Ask only for the information necessary to process an order. People are unlikely to make a repeat purchase if they have to write out their autobiography before they have their order processed.

E-mail and customer support

E-mail remains the most popular application on the Internet and as such is likely to be the electronic medium your customers are most familiar with. As we have discussed elsewhere in this book, e-mail can be a great way of consolidating your brand identity as it enables you to send out newsletters to people who have subscribed to your mailing list. E-mail can also be used to great effect as a sales support tool. It can take the two-way relationship between your site and its customer base to a deeper, more personal level. Here are some of the areas and techniques you should consider when using e-mail for customer support purposes.

Delivery notification

Once an order has been placed at your Web site, at least one e-mail message should be sent out confirming the order. Many companies send out an e-mail at various intervals between the moment the order is processed and when the product arrives at the customer's doorstep. Amazon, for instance, not only e-mails its customers when an order has been confirmed and when a product is delivered, but also to tell them when their product has left the Amazon warehouse.

Update notices

E-mail can be used to tell existing customers and mailing list subscribers when your site, products or services are updated.

Advice

As we have discovered, the range of products or services you offer online needs to be supplemented with useful information. E-mail can be used in conjunction with your site, to provide free advice relating to your products and services.

Customer enquiries

Unless they are made in discussion groups or other online forums, customer enquiries should be responded to via e-mail. When responding to customer enquiries you must be sure to answer queries as quickly as possible. Owing to the 'type-click-deliver' nature of e-mail, people generally expect responses within 24 hours.

Use a file library of responses

Responding to messages within 24 hours may not be an option if you are writing each message individually. Therefore, if people are requiring the same information, set up a file library of responses to FAQs and respond to each similar message with a cut-and-pasted pre-prepared response.

Use automatic response software

If you find answering messages by hand is too time-consuming (even with a file library of responses) you may need to think about getting an automatic response software program (your ISP is likely to offer one). This will help you set up different mailboxes for different types of messages and set up the software to respond automatically with a different reply for each mailbox. Response software such as Brightware (www.brightware.com), Aweber (www.aweber.com) and Echo Mail (www.echomail.com) offer you a way to respond to infinite incoming e-mails as they arrive in your mailbox. A computer response may not be ideal but it is better than no response at all. Until recently, it was quite commonplace for e-mail requests and feedback to web sites to be unanswered or ignored. Nowadays, the software available enables you to preset criteria so that people get a more personalized response than a mere acknowledgement of receipt.

Increasing product value

According to a study conducted by the Centre for Research in Electronic Commerce at the University of Texas, which looked at over 1200 companies in Europe and the USA, real world companies that use the Internet as a customer service tool do a lot better financially than those that don't. Company Web sites that not only enable customers to place and modify orders in a secure online environment, but also notify customers of their order status *and* provide product recommendations based on their previous purchases, perhaps unsurprisingly, fared better than those companies that use the Internet solely as a promotional tool. (The study, titled 'E-Business Value Assessment' is discussed in further detail in Chapter 13.)

It is not enough, however, simply to sell products on your site. To get people to buy from your Web site rather than from your online and offline competition, you need to induce visitors with more than just an electronic sales catalogue. Here are some of the ways to add value to the products you offer.

Customer endorsements

Endorsements from customers who have tried and tested products are always going to be more effective than meaningless advertising statements. Amazon's book reviews are a prime example of the power of the interactive customer testimonial.

Discounts

The Internet has brought with it the age of comparative shopping. Customers can hunt out the cheapest price for a product with greater ease than ever before. They can visit around 10 similar sites within a half hour period via the major search engines and even ask around in the thousands of consumer-focused online discussion groups indexed at DejaNews (www.deja.com). Companies that can differentiate themselves by offering the biggest discounts and the lowest prices will find the visitor-customer conversion an easier task.

Personalization

The Internet enables you to personalize the relationship you have with each customer by keeping a record of his or her shopping activity. Once you know what a customer has bought before, it becomes possible to anticipate what he or she may be likely to buy in the future. This means you can recommend products which, based on their former purchases, could interest them. Various e-commerce software tools offer 'customer profiling' features, enabling you to target promotions and products for registered customers.

Interaction

Online forums such as discussion groups and chat rooms can generate conversation between customers at your site. This means other customers can take your place as sales representatives when 'newbies' (first-time visitors) ask for product advice.

Cross-selling

Various e-commerce 'shop in a box' packages (such as Intershop) allow you to cross-sell different products. This is where complementary products are promoted based on customer behaviour.

Expert advice

By offering the chance to provide expert purchasing advice (as opposed to biased sales jargon), the Internet enables you to give customers more in-depth information about a product than they would normally encounter in the real world.

Case study: Amazon.com. Database marketing

Amazon.com *knows* its customers. It uses the Web's ability to document itself to record customer activity. This information is then used to add value to the overall customer experience. Customers are greeted personally with something similar to the following message: 'Hello, Kate Brown. Based on the items you've bought at Amazon.com, we think you'll like these. This list changes daily, so check back often.'

Amazon.com uses a database engine to keep a log of the purchases made by its millions of customers. Almost instantaneously, a tailored list of recommendations appears on the screen as regular customers arrive at the site. Even new visitors feel the benefit of Amazon.com's database technology. When someone is viewing a book or CD, a list of other recommendations appears based on what other people have bought. Furthermore, users can access reviews posted by other customers before they make a purchase.

When it comes to ordering, Amazon.com, as with many other successful e-tailers, deploys the 'shopping-cart' method. This means users can add any number of products to an electronic holding area (the 'shopping cart') and swap or change products at any time prior to purchase. Amazon.com takes the ordering process to the next level by keeping a full shopping history of each customer that can be used each time a customer makes a new order. Furthermore, Amazon.com simplifies and speeds up the whole process through its patented 'one-click shopping' system.

When it comes to security Amazon.com not only uses a secure server, but also takes the trouble to explain how it works and why it is safe. Acknowledging that many e-shopper virgins may still remain sceptical, Amazon.com also provides the option of giving credit card details over the phone. Customers are put further at ease once they have placed the order, as an order confirmation is sent automatically via e-mail. This is by no means the only time Amazon contacts its customers via e-mail. It also uses e-mail to send out notifications of product shipments, recommendations, reviews, customer surveys and electronic receipts. All of this adds to the impression of a business that not only knows what the customer wants, but also how to deliver it.

Fulfilment

A survey conducted by US Internet research company eMarketer found that the biggest causes of customer frustration are (in descending order):

- out-of-stock merchandise;
- late (or no) delivery;
- poor Web site performance;
- huge or hidden shipping rates.

If your Web site is guilty of any of the above then unhappy customers are an inevitable consequence. Furthermore, owing to the phenomenal speed with which word of Web travels, this ensures that your site's performance will be heard about by people who haven't experienced it first hand. 'If a customer has a bad experience in a bricks-and-mortar shop, they will tell about five people', says Phil Walker, managing director of Dublin-based Internet consultancy Ebeon. 'If they have a bad one on the Internet, they can tell 50 or 50,000 by posting it up on a Web message board.' Fulfilment, in an e-marketing context, not only refers to being able to provide customers with products on time and as requested, it also means building long-lasting and mutually beneficial relationships with customers.

Summary

According to market research organization Mintel, 'the balance of power in the e-economy has shifted towards the consumer'. On the Internet, 'consumers expect superior customer service and this is an area where online retailers must differentiate themselves from their offline counterparts' (from 'UK vs US Online Shopping Report, Retail Intelligence', June 2000). It is no longer enough simply to rely on the strength of your products or services alone. You must also be able to fulfil the newly formed expectations of your online customers. You must also concentrate on the shopping process itself, to ensure that customers will not only complete their orders but will also return to your site to make repeat purchases.

ten

Brand building on the **Internet**

While in the real world building a brand may seem like an extravagance best left to the multinationals, on the Internet even the smallest companies have to create a strong brand identity. In fact, many marketers have successfully argued that the smaller the business, the stronger the brand has to be. As Jennifer Praeger comments on the Ad Resource Web site: 'If you don't spend the money on branding, then the only criterion left is price.' A larger company will almost always have the advantage of competing solely on price. The other reason branding is important is *differentiation*: after all, without an identity that is different to your competitors what incentive do people have to visit your site? Of course, in the real world, people may shop with you because you are closer to where they live, but on the Internet physical factors such as geography count for little.

This chapter aims to provide some insight into the unique nature of branding on the Internet, as well as give you some useful pointers for developing your own e-brand.

The importance of e-branding

The significance of branding online is set to increase further owing to the changing habits of net users. Already many people are predicting the ultimate demise of 'surfing' on the Internet, as users head direct for the brands they know and trust. Benoit Wiesser, planning consultant with branding consultancy CLK, says: 'Mature Internet users frequently visit just 10 or 12 sites and only have a real affinity with perhaps one or two of those. Dot coms have got to own a customer base and to do that they need to go beyond just selling their wares. They need to build communities.'

Another challenge facing businesses on the Internet is the exponential growth in the number of Web sites competing for attention. A few years ago one of the keys to successful Internet branding was niche marketing. If you could provide a unique product or service you would get visitors for the simple reason that no one else was doing it. Nowadays, however, there are hardly any new niches to exploit. Unless you are planning to set up a site for cross-dressing yak-farmers who enjoy karaoke, you will not be alone in cyberspace. This means your brand identity needs to be as distinctive as possible in order to stand out in an increasingly overcrowded digital marketplace.

Brand misconceptions

Branding is one of the most misunderstood concepts of the Internet age. Before establishing exactly what branding *is*, it is important to clear up what it is *not*. Here are three of the most common misconceptions:

- *Awareness*. When people talk about branding what they are often talking about is awareness. In the late 1990s an e-brand's success would often be measured in terms of how many people had visited a Web site or seen a banner ad. It soon became apparent, however, that creating loyalty among existing customers was more cost-effective than constantly hunting for new ones.
- *Advertising*. Although the words 'branding' and 'advertising' are often used interchangeably, they are not the same thing. Advertising is only one of the many tools that can be used to express the brand message; it is not the brand itself.
- *A logo*. There is more to branding than having an eye-catching logo, a great strap line or a slick Web site.

Defining a brand

A brand can be defined in many ways. Marketing practitioners often talk about a brand as an attitude, a set of values, a look, an idea or even a way of life. The easiest way to view a brand, however, is as an association. When someone thinks about your company, they are in fact thinking about your brand identity. In other words, a brand is not a product or service but the qualities associated with the products or services a company offers. Therefore, the brand identity of, say, Volvo is not the cars themselves but the more abstract notion of 'safety'.

Companies that embrace the branding phenomenon emphasize these product or service attributes in their marketing campaigns. IBM, for instance, doesn't talk in terms of computer hardware but in terms of 'solutions'. The gap between the brand message and the product or service is most apparent in companies that have a strong and consistent brand identity, despite offering a wide range of contrasting products. Virgin is perhaps the most obvious example of this type of brand. According to Richard Branson, the aim is to 'build brands not around products but around reputation'. While reputation is important offline, on the Internet, as we will see, it is everything.

Ultimately, you must acknowledge that the idea of a 'brand' is bigger than the Web site or product itself.

The anatomy of a brand

The collective brand image of your business is comprised of various elements. Obviously the products or services you offer affect the way people view your brand, but there are also many other factors that can have a strong impact. These include:

- *Domain names.* As we shall discuss towards the end of this chapter, the choice of domain name (or names) has a direct effect on a company or Web site's brand identity.
- *Web site design.* The way a Web site is designed obviously helps define the identity of a brand in the mind of a customer. While the visual elements (such as the colour scheme, type font, logo design and so on) are important, what really matters is *usability*. Usability is the Internet buzzword relating to the functional aspects of Web design such as navigation, download times and organization.
- *Customer service.* Good customer service is essential if you are to achieve a positive brand identity. On the Internet, the customer comes first or the company finishes last. Amazon and other successful online companies have built their entire brand around the notion of customer service.

■ *Community*. Almost without exception, the leading online brands are also successful communities. Yahoo!, Amazon, eBay, Napster, AOL, CDNow – all of these companies have built communities around their Web sites which have helped develop and sustain an effective brand identity. Sites that can build communities can also build the two most sought after brand virtues: trust and loyalty.

The e-branding difference

The Internet brings with it an entirely new way of branding products, services and companies. As Niall Fitzgerald, chairman of Unilever, told the European Association of Advertising Agencies in a keynote speech, 'one-way, mass-communication has its best and biggest days behind it'. For brands to survive and succeed in an age of interactivity, a completely new approach is necessary. Below are some of the ways the Internet has revolutionized the nature of branding.

Consumer choice

Whereas for the industrial age choice meant any colour so long as it's black, on the Internet users are presented with a kaleidoscopic range of possibilities. When Brand X fails to deliver, Brand Y is always only one click away. After all, if someone is visiting a site from a search engine (and most people do) they are likely to have a list of 10 or so other sites they want to visit.

Faster development

Because the Web is self-documenting it is easy for online brands to discover what works and what doesn't. Net software can help businesses track not only which Web pages prove the most popular but also how visitors are getting there (even providing details of which keywords are typed into a search engine). This means that companies can develop and market sites around the consumer without having to resort to traditional research methods. Brands can develop faster, mistakes can be rectified quicker and the brand message itself evolves into a mutually beneficial conversation.

Brand depth

As the Internet progresses there is a move away from thinking about 'eyeballs' to a concentration on relationships. Many leading e-business figures now believe brand development should be measured less in terms of how quickly a site can expand its customer base and more in terms of how existing customers decide to come back.

As Rory Sutherland, executive creative director of OgilvyOne has put it: 'The Internet is about brand depth, not breadth. It's not worth chasing share of market, it's share of wallet that really counts. Once you have your loyal community, there are fabulous opportunities for cross-selling, personalized services and meeting the multiple needs of the same group.'

Networked markets

Not only does the Internet enable companies and their customers to engage in conversation with each other, but it also helps customers to talk to other customers about your company. As the Cluetrain Web site explains, 'Markets are conversations. Through the Internet, people are discovering and inventing new ways to share relevant knowledge with blinding speed. As a direct result, markets are getting smarter – and getting smarter faster than most companies.'

Brand feedback

Prolific e-brands such as Amazon, eBay, QXL, Yahoo! and MSN have learnt that if visitors communicate with each other, it not only increases their loyalty to a site (and hence their 'lifetime value') but it also enables the brand to develop in line with the needs of the consumer by providing visitors with a platform on which they can voice their opinions on the brand. In some cases opinions aired in community forums have led to a radical rethinking of e-companies' marketing strategies.

For instance, when Amazon was toying with the idea of variable pricing, it decided to trial run the policy for one week on its DVD products only. Amazon then monitored its DVD Talk chat forum to try and gauge consumer response. When it spotted a handful of negative comments Amazon immediately announced that it was withdrawing the policy because, in the words of Amazon's chief executive Jeff Bezos, 'it created uncertainty for customers rather than simplifying their lives'. Amazon was therefore able to act quickly, before it became too heavily associated with what was appearing to be an unpopular move.

Brand democracy

Due to the democratic nature of the Internet, even the smallest of companies can eventually become the biggest brands. This is because having a unique approach is far more effective than spending millions on online and offline advertising. Furthermore, because of the immediacy of the Internet the value of a great concept can be spread around the world in a matter of minutes.

Uncovering your brand

Before you can promote your online brand, you need to work out exactly what you are promoting. Far too many companies have suffered from embarking on expensive or time-intensive advertising campaigns without taking the time necessary to develop a brand identity. This only leads to a fragmented and disjointed message that confuses rather than inspires potential customers. To make sure your marketing activity makes the maximum impact, you need to be clear of your brand identity from the outset. This involves defining the personality of your company and working out how this personality should translate to the Internet. Here are some guidelines to consider when you attempt to uncover your unique brand identity.

Be honest

On the Internet, the true picture of a company will always emerge. It therefore makes no sense to try and paint an unrealistic picture of your company. After all, if customers cannot get an authentic picture of your company from your Web site, they will be able to find it elsewhere.

Be consistent

Once you have uncovered your brand identity, every part of your online activity should reflect the personality of your brand. From the visual layout of your Web site to the way you write your e-mails, nothing should go against the grain of your values.

Think of superlatives

As the main point of branding is to differentiate your business from its competitors, it is helpful to think of superlatives that can apply to your brand. If you were the first or fastest to do something, for instance, this could be used as the foundation for what Kevin Roberts, CEO of Saatchi and Saatchi US, refers to as the 'mythology of the brand'.

Think of other superlatives that could be used as your unique selling point. If you are the biggest, smallest, most popular, cheapest, most expensive or longest running within your industry, your brand objective should be to shout about the fact. Mediocrity is the enemy of the online brand, so anything that makes your site unique should be embraced.

Think from the outside in

As we have discussed elsewhere in this book, thinking from the outside in (that is to say, from the perspective of your customers and other audiences) is key to e-marketing success. As B L Ochman has observed on the Web Review site, 'the user experience is your brand'.

Be patient

Although the Internet is a fast paced medium, it still takes some time to brand your business successfully. This is due to the fact that trust and loyalty cannot be built overnight, but rather have to be earned by consistently satisfying the customer's needs.

The e-branding paradox

In her exemplary critique of branding, *No Logo*, Naomi Klein discusses the Internet's ability to generate 'pure brands'. 'It is online that the purest brands are being built', she claims. 'These brands are free to soar, less as the disseminators of goods or services than as collective hallucinations.'

However, this is only half the story. As Klein herself acknowledges, the Internet provides consumers with a means of not only talking back to companies, but also of talking to each other. If someone has a complaint against a brand, they can share that complaint with hundreds of others in online discussion groups, message boards and consumer opinion sites. This means that online brands become more associated with the reality of the customer's experience than ever before, even though they are less confined by real world constraints such as geography. If your brand message diverges from what your customers are saying to each other elsewhere on the Web, then your brand is in trouble. The plethora of anti-sites such as BritishScareways and Microsucks, as well as the infinite number of customer complaint-based discussion groups, provides clear evidence of the power of customer feedback online. The way to make sure your brand message evolves in line with the experience of your customers is to incorporate customer opinion within your online activity. The most effective way of doing this is to develop a community around your site.

Online communities

Whether you have a highly specialized business-to-business site, or a games site aimed at children, online communities can help you achieve your marketing goals.

As relationships are the foundation stone upon which all other e-marketing objectives are built, communities built around a single cause add value to your site from the perspective of both your business and its customers. After all, you can spend six-figure sums on advertising, but it won't buy you the loyalty and profitability of a few very committed customers.

As Matt Perry from Internet marketing firm Net Marketeers explains: 'Sites which build online communities are clearly going to have an advantage over static, one-way sites when it comes to brand development. Interactive questionnaires, discussion areas, and straightforward contact links can all help steer a marketing campaign in the right direction and keep companies up-to-date with the latest word of Web.'

The core components of an online community are:

- a shared purpose;
- a sense of trust, including reputations and boundaries;
- a mutual history;
- an overview;
- enhanced interaction.

To build an effective online community around your site it is important to look at each of these individual components in turn.

A shared purpose

Communities centre on a common purpose that unifies the group. If you cannot offer people a real and compelling reason to come together, and if you cannot enable people within the community to achieve something in line with this purpose, then your community will be doomed to failure.

According to Cynthia Typaldos, President and CEO of the US-based Real Communities, 'There's a big difference between people who have a shared purpose and people who merely have something in common. You can't build a community around people who own white cars, for example.' Cynthia cites the example of Citibank, a company that tried to create a community around its checking-account customers. 'But what's the common purpose or the shared passion among checking-account customers? They're just a random group of people who happen to have checking accounts at Citibank.'

It therefore doesn't matter how many digital tools you use to form an online community, if your community fails to have clarity of purpose you will face a struggle to get it off the ground. You also need to ensure that this purpose is directly relevant to your Web site. For instance, if you sell tennis equipment you could set up a community for people committed to improving their tennis skills. If you provide financial services, a community based around the shared purpose of finding solid investment advice would be appropriate.

Many companies are now realizing it may be more cost-effective to worry less about attracting thousands of new customers, and think more about how to get more out of their existing ones. In other words, repeat traffic is starting to be considered as being as (if not more) important as attracting 'virgin visitors'. E-businesses are now focused on a customer's 'lifetime value' and are therefore thinking of how to hold on to them for the long term. The solution, as many see it, lies in converting a Web site into a community. As a comprehensive study conducted by US research organization Consumer Reports concluded, online communities are the most effective way to take an e-business 'back to its roots' as a consumer-driven organization.

The so-called 'network effect' which an online community creates can become the driving force behind a Web site, attracting new visitors while at the same time making existing customers more loyal. This last point is especially important. Active community members are likely also to be active customers.

Particpate.com is a company that provides technology and consulting services for online community management. It has discovered first-hand that community members are the most valued type of online customer. As Participate.com's President and CEO, Adam Warms explains: 'A consumer site we worked with found that people who participated in its community bought six times more merchandise than casual visitors.'

There are various tools that can convert a Web site into a Web community. These include discussion groups, e-mailing lists, chat rooms and interactive newsletters. Software alone, however, is not enough. To make your community 'real', you will also have to think of the factors common to all communities; these are discussed below.

A sense of trust

Trust is, of course, an essential element of all e-marketing activity. For instance, people are unlikely to type in their credit card details if a Web site doesn't have a secure server. When it comes to communities however, the issue of trust is not just dependent on you, but on every member of the community.

For trust to be built, people within the community must have consistent identities. Members need to be able to recognize each other.

Reputations
Linked with identity and trust is the idea of reputation. Successful community sites enable members to assess the value of other members' contributions.

On Amazon.com, arguably the most effective community-minded Web site, people can actually vote on how helpful they found another member's book or CD review to be. Another leading e-brand that believes firmly in the notion of dot communities is eBay (see Figure 10.1). At the site, members can rate the quality of their experience with other members, and those opinions are then converted into a star ranking for each member. The ultimate ranking is a shooting star. To be worthy of this you need 10,000 positive feedback postings from the community. This clearly gives people an incentive to keep coming back to the site once they have received a certain amount of positive postings. As Cynthia Typaldos says, 'If a community has a way of awarding status that is visible to other members, people will strive to achieve it.'

Boundaries

Although you may want a lot of people to be a part of your online community, you need to set barriers to entry. It doesn't take a

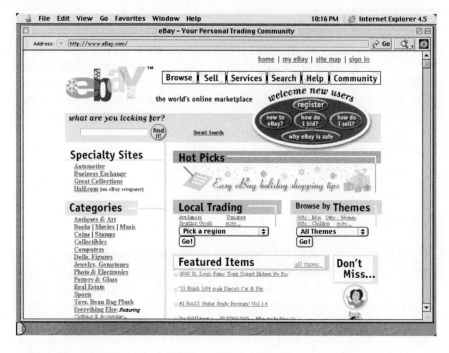

Figure 10.1 eBay Web site. Auction site eBay has one of the strongest online communities on the web

degree in sociology to appreciate that half of being 'a part of' something is about being 'apart from' something else. Another reason to have boundaries is to make sure members take an active role. This all helps strengthen solidarity within the group. In the real world these boundaries are often geographical and do not have to be enforced. On the Internet, however, geography does not exist and so the set boundaries need to relate to the group's shared purpose. This could be in the form of a quiz or test relating to the topic.

If you do not want to stop people from taking part in the main area of your site, you could set up an exclusive 'members only' sub-area, which can only be accessed with a password. This is done to great effect by London-based nightclub and record label Ministry of Sound. Fitting with the idea of a nightclub, its Web site includes a 'VIP Room', a registration-only area that entitles members to privileges such as free music downloads and access to exclusive information.

A mutual history

A sense of history is integral to any community, either online or offline. If you have a discussion group or other communication-building forum it is important to make sure new members can see how the group has evolved over time by keeping a record of messages. Specialized community software can ensure that events and postings appear in reverse chronological order.

In addition to the above criteria, online communities should also provide an overview and enhanced interaction.

An overview

While in the real world it is only possible to know about a tiny section of a community, on the Internet a complete overview can always be achieved. Members should be able to know what topics are currently being discussed, which members are taking part, how many new members there are, which messages have been posted most recently, and so on. Any other information that affects the present situation of the community as a whole should be included.

Enhanced interaction

Communities are built on relationships and, as has been pointed out elsewhere in this book, strong relationships depend on interaction. The more interactivity is encouraged between fellow members, the greater the community bond will be.

Domain names

A rose by any other name may smell as sweet, but when it comes to brand building naming is everything. The strength of your domain name can set your site apart from its competitors and lead to the ultimate e-branding goal: differentiation. Below are some suggestions for when you are considering a new domain name.

Make sure your name translates well

If you are targeting a global audience, you need to ensure that your name holds no negative implications in different languages. Evite.com, for instance, was puzzled by its poor reception in many parts of the globe after spending millions on promoting its party Web site worldwide. It had failed to realize that 'evite' is the root of the word 'avoid' in all the Romance languages. Internet users in countries such as France, Italy, Spain, Portugal and Argentina consequently stayed clear of the Web site.

Make sure it is easy to spell

The longer and more complex your domain name, the harder it will be for your customers to type it in correctly.

Keep it short

Short domain names are preferable to long ones as they take less time for visitors to type and tend to be easier to remember. Of course, if you are after a .com suffix there are very few effective short names left for the taking, so some imagination may be needed to come up with something short, memorable and available.

Make it self-explanatory

As virtually every market sector is represented by thousands of Web sites it makes sense to have a domain name that gets to the point and, to use the old expression, 'does exactly what it says on the tin'. Company names such as Letsbuyit.com, NextWeekend.com and Cheapbeer.com clearly fall into this category. If your company is a traditional bricks and mortar operation it may make more sense to stick with your offline name (no matter how dry and boring it is). You can purchase a more 'to the point' name to use in advertising campaigns.

Buy more than one domain name

There are several reasons why you should purchase alternative domain names. The main one of course is to avoid potential confusion on the part of your customers with your business or site name. If, say, your original domain name ended with the .co.uk suffix you should at least purchase the .com suffix as well (and possibly .net). Also, if you have a name that can be spelt in various ways you should get hold of each variant spelling. This will prevent competitors from taking advantage and help you preserve the individuality of your brand or trademark names.

The power of the domain name is illustrated by the many companies that have found that one of the easiest ways to change your brand identity is to change your domain name. For instance, the British-based free music site MP3.co.uk changed its name to SkipMusic.co.uk, following the growing controversy surrounding MP3 technology (which had been accused of encouraging copyright infringement). This name change led to a more legitimate brand identity, which helped gain the company favour with the record industry. Likewise, the customized news service Mercury Mail changed its name to InfoBeat to give the company an up-to-the-minute feel that would prove more attractive to its target audience.

Learning from successful brands

To get an idea of how the Web can be used to build an effective and distinctive brand identity, it is helpful to look at companies that have embraced the Internet on its own terms. All of the sites listed below have managed to successfully brand themselves by finding a point of differentiation between them and their competition. Furthermore, most of them have managed to find a way of incorporating the user's experience into the brand message itself.

Procter and Gamble: Physique (www.physique.com)

Procter and Gamble is another one of the companies that is starting to come round to the virtues of cyber branding. It decided to launch its newest hair-care product, 'Physique' with a Web-intensive campaign. Having spent a phenomenal 70 per cent of its promotional budget on the Internet, Physique had soon became one of P&G's most visited sites, with over 500,000 people having subscribed to an online community called the 'Physique club'. This online community provides P&G with valuable feedback as customers exchange comments on different products in the range, while at the same time ensuring a strong core of loyal customers.

Allied Domecq: Dunkin Donuts (www.dunkin donuts.org)

When Dunkin Donuts discovered a hostile consumer opinion site at www.dunkindonuts.org it decided to join in the conversation, correcting misinformation as it did so. Instead of ignoring the site Dunkin Donuts actively encouraged its store managers to monitor it and respond to criticism as politely as possible. Allied Domecq, Dunkin Donuts' parent company, then decided to buy the site from David Felton (the aggrieved customer who originally set up the anti-site) to use as a consumer feedback mechanism which Felton still presides over.

Amazon (www.amazon.com – .co.uk)

There are many e-branding lessons to learn from Amazon. Perhaps the most important is its outside-in approach. From the outset it built its brand around the needs of its customers. This is evident in its continued ability to alleviate consumer fears surrounding security and fulfilment, in its patented 'one-click shopping' system, in its move towards a diversified 'one-stop-shop' model, and its bottom-up pricing structures. Amazon, like Yahoo! and eBay, has also benefited from having what Silicon Valley types deem the ultimate brand bonus: *first mover advantage.* As an online bookstore Amazon became big first and fast, driven by the strong marketing vision and foresight of co-founder Jeff Bezos.

Worldpop.com (www.worldpop.com)

Worldpop.com, one of the world's leading pop music sites, refers to itself as 'the global pop network'. Its home page includes links to 'chat', 'messages' and 'community' sections alongside 'interviews', 'tickets', 'news', 'games' and 'charts' links (see Figure 10.2).

Using the strap line, 'Your world, your music', Worldpop's aim is clearly to achieve a community feel, with some areas exclusive to

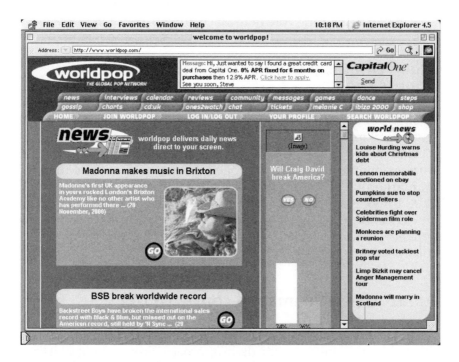

Figure 10.2 Worldpop.com Web site. Worldpop.com has built a community by valuing and encouraging interaction between its visitors

members as well as a chat room or message board. Visitors are asked to submit their own thoughts on albums, music videos and concerts, which further increases the interactivity on the site.

Although the site's community is aimed squarely at its target consumer market, it doesn't ignore its other audiences. For instance, the bottom left of the home page invites you to click 'for advertising and other commercial opportunities'. This takes visitors to a separate business-to-business section, providing a list of useful e-mail and phone contacts for sponsorship, marketing, record industry services, advertising, promotions and content.

Brand aid

There are a lot of online resources that can help you in your quest to create a distinctive e-brand identity. Here are some of the best:

- *Cluetrain (www.cluetrain.com).* The Cluetrain Web site offers a provocative and intelligent look at the way the Internet changes the nature of business, brands and marketing.
- *Wilson Web* (www.wilsonweb.com). As one of the best marketing Web sites around, Wilson Web provides a mine of information relating to online brand building. It could also be worthwhile signing up for the Web Marketing Today fortnightly newsletter, which occasionally provides practical advice on Internet branding.
- *EMarketeer* (www.emarketeer.com). This long established site not only provides useful information on all aspects of Internet marketing, but also a discussion forum populated by e-marketing experts. This could therefore be a useful place to seek personal and professional advice on your online brands.
- *ClickZ* (www.clickz.com). A very popular e-zine with articles on branding, advertising and marketing in general from a US perspective.

Summary

As people are increasingly only visiting the sites they know and trust, distinctive branding is essential on the Internet. Furthermore, the fact that the Internet enables closer interaction between a business and its market means that brands can become more centred on the requirements of the end user. It also means brands can go further in adding to the customer's 'lifetime value' than ever before. This can only be done successfully, however, if you make every effort to create a clear brand identity from the outset. This does not mean that you need to spend lots of money on generating awareness through advertising campaigns and sponsorship deals. What it does mean is that you need to take the time to understand what makes your site or company unique, and also to appreciate why Internet users would want to visit you rather than your competition. As the number of Web sites reaches saturation point, figuring out this point of difference is becoming ever more essential.

eleven

Advertising
online

Advertising is the area of Internet marketing that causes the most debate. Many marketers believe that paid-for online advertising is the least effective means of getting a company's message across, while others believe it is crucial for long-term survival. This chapter will begin by putting the cases for and against Internet advertising before taking a look in more depth at the most popular methods.

The case for online advertising

Supporters of e-advertising methods claim that low click-through rates on banner ads hardly mean anything. Furthermore, they have a mine of evidence to bolster their case. For instance, an Andersen Consulting survey of nearly 2000 experienced Internet users found that banner ads are generally more effective than print or broadcast adverts in terms of winning over new shoppers. According to the survey, banners were the driving force for 25 per cent of users to shop online, whereas newspaper and magazine ads incited only 14 per cent spend money via the Internet.

When refined targeting techniques are added into the equation, e-advertising can prove even more effective. Now it is possible (provided the budget is big enough) to tailor ads based on the Internet user's most recent online activity. This means if someone has just bought a computer over the net, it is possible to remove the banner that promoted this purchase and put in its place an ad for a printer or scanner. E-auction sites such as eBay and QXL have pioneered this tailored approach by updating the message content of Web and e-mail-based ads according to the current auction item and even the latest bid price.

Advances are also being made in the way online advertising is being measured. Measuring click-through rates is now considered an outmoded and inaccurate way of judging an ad's success. Various studies from authoritative sources such as the Internet Advertising Bureau have confirmed that around 80 per cent of ad-related actions are not based on clicks. As online adman Neve Savage remarked in *Marketing Week*, 'there is rarely a correlation between clicks and sales: indeed, the correlation is often inverse. Building an online ad campaign on click data alone will lead to entirely the wrong decisions'. Online advertising can now be measured right the way through to the sale or action.

The other argument in support of spending money on Internet advertising is the fact that more and more major advertisers are choosing the net as their advertising medium of choice. For instance, when Procter and Gamble launched its new hair care product, Physique, it invested 70 per cent of its advertising budget on the Web and the remainder of it on TV. Other companies have gone even further in this direction. Volvo supported the US launch of its S60 saloon entirely online. Similarly Ford has launched various new models in the US by capitalizing on the 'network effect' online advertising can create. At the other end of the scale, growing numbers of smaller 'clicks and mortar' companies are using cost-effective forms of online advertising, such as banner exchanges. Furthermore, while print and broadcast media are benefiting from expensive advertising campaigns promoting Internet-based companies such as Yahoo! and AOL, traditional real world campaigns (both large and small) are moving away from the magazines, radio and TV advertising in favour of cyberspace. Forester Research expects the online advertising market to rocket to a phenomenal total of $33 billion by 2004.

The case against online advertising

One of the strongest cases against e-advertising is the fact that free marketing methods often prove more effective. There is certainly no denying that as most net users arriving at a site for the first time do so via a search engine, a high search engine position generally brings more rewards than a flashy banner ad. In light of this, David Weinberger, co-author of the highly influential *Cluetrain Manifesto*, poses the rhetorical question: 'Why get someone to look at an ad on the Web when, with exactly the same amount of wrist power, you can get them into your electronic storefront itself?'

Another argument against online advertising centres on the decline in click-through rates. Whereas a few years ago a banner ad would typically be clicked-through by between 5 and 10 per cent of net users, nowadays click-through rates are continually below 1 per cent. There are, it is believed, two contributing factors involved in this decline. First and foremost, there is the growing cynicism of Internet users who increasingly see banners as an irritating distraction from the information they are really after. Secondly, more and more users are setting their Web browsers to ignore banners, so many people are simply not seeing the banners that advertisers have tailored for them. Therefore, while both sides of the e-advertising fence agree that click-through rates in themselves no longer provide a valid means of assessment, critics claim that the *decline* in these rates is symptomatic of an increased scepticism about banner ads.

The strongest and most radical argument against online advertising, however, concerns the two-way nature of the Internet itself. As Internet guru Esther Dyson stated in a seminar at the London Business School, 'Things are two-way now. Customers are talking back to companies, employers are talking back to their bosses and vendors are talking back to suppliers.' Advertising, on the other hand is, a one-way tool. That is to say, the person watching, reading or even clicking on the advert doesn't interact with its message. As Brent Marshall from San Francisco based e-marketing firm Logic First puts it, 'Internet marketing is about conversation and dialogue whereas advertising is, by its very nature, a monologue. Furthermore, however much money is spent on advertising a company via the Internet, the real picture will always emerge.'

On the Internet the truth is always 'out there', but it doesn't take an X-Files agent to uncover consumer or client opinion. Usenet news groups (which can be searched by company name), e-mail-based discussion groups and sites such as Planet Feedback and eComplaints all provide customers with the opportunity to present their first-hand experiences of a company in front of a receptive audience. Increasing numbers of potential online shoppers are turning to these types of online resources to ask for recommendations or advice before making their purchase. Therefore, while an ad may tell you 'our service is unbeatable', a member of a newsgroup may also tell you about the company's poor delivery record and lax security standards. In the words of Doc Searles, who co-founded one of Silicon Valley's leading advertising agencies, 'What these little voices used to say to a single friend is now accessible to the world, and so the market conversation punctures the exaggerations made in an ad. The speed of word of mouth is now limited only by how fast people can type.'

Therefore, according to its critics, online advertising is an unwelcome confirmation of Marshall McLuhan's belief that new forms of media always bring with them ill-fitting remnants of the old media. While advertising is perfectly suited to the offline media, they argue, it is undermined by the interactions that occur in cyberspace. The logic of this argument leads to the following conclusion: the Internet's central purpose as an information resource both undermines, and is itself undermined by, the singularity and one-sided nature of advertising campaigns.

The verdict

When set against offline advertising, the arguments in favour of ad spend on the Internet are clear. While advertisers offline cannot guarantee that they are reaching people who buy online, when they advertise on the net this clearly is not a problem.

While banner advertising can be a good way of getting people to see your domain name and generating awareness of your Web site, it is not so effective in leading to direct sales.

For big companies, generating awareness is often enough, at least for the short term. Companies such as Amazon, Jungle and CDNow have spent fortunes advertising online simply to boost the profile of their brands. This 'profile first, profits last' game often works well for the Internet Goliaths, but it is less of an option for the average small to medium-sized business. That's not to say online advertising won't work, it's just that it needs to be very carefully researched and targeted.

Ultimately, the success of online advertising depends on your site. For some sites, banners may not be effective; for others, they are still producing results. Before rushing headlong into a 'hook, line and sinker' ad campaign, test the water by initially committing only a tiny fraction of your promotional budget or even by trying out one of the free banner exchanges.

Banner ads

Despite ongoing debate over the usefulness of banner ads they remain a ubiquitous presence on the Web. Visit any search engine, portal or other popular site and the chances are you will be bombarded by kaleidoscopic, flashing banners either enticing or irritating you with invitations to an eclectic range of Web sites. Banner ads have been described as the billboards of the information superhighway but actually they are more like road signs, directing people to online locations they may never have heard of before.

Banners can be static or interactive and can incorporate both text and images. Typically they provide a hypertext link to the advertiser's home page, enabling users to click through the banner. Click-through rates vary widely depending on how targeted a company's banners are. Similarly, the cost of placing banner ads changes significantly from site to site.

Although there is no set right or wrong way to design a banner, the use of animation, teaser questions and direct instructions (such as 'Enter our site here') tends to improve click-through rates. If you are designing a banner ad yourself you will need to use a graphic design software package such as Macromedia Fireworks or Adobe PhotoShop. Visit Web Review (www.webreview.com) for reviews of the latest banner ad design tools. The more specific the banner is, the more likely it is that clicks will be able to be converted into sales. For more information on how to design a banner ad visit Ads Guide (www.ad-guide.com; see Figure 11.1), which also provides a searchable subject index of everything related to online advertising.

Banner economics

If you want banner ads to boost sales rather than simply consolidate brand awareness, you will need to look carefully at how much banner advertising will cost you. Banner advertising worked out on a CPM rate (cost per thousand – see below) can certainly prove expensive. For instance, a standard CPM rate is about $10/£6. If you then consider the average click-through rate (0.4–0.6 per cent) in conjunction with the average click-to-sale conversion rate of 2 per cent, you can see that you will have to pay for a lot of page impressions before you can guarantee a sale. Therefore, while the

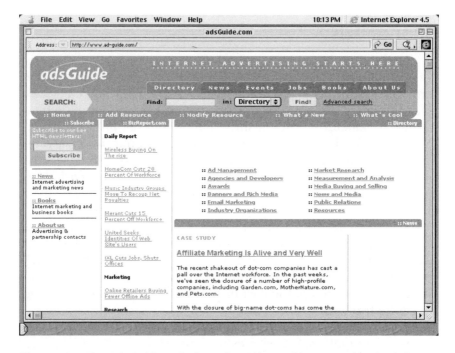

Figure 11.1 The Ads Guide Web site. Ads Guide provides comprehensive information on banner advertising

click-through rate is relatively straightforward to measure, the most significant measure you need to look at is cost per sale.

Banner exchanges

The easiest, and certainly the cheapest way to go about advertising your site online is to take part in one of the many banner exchange programs out there. The way they work is simple. You go to one of the banner exchange sites and sign up for the service. You then submit a banner that advertises your site (usually 468 pixels wide by 60 pixels high). This banner will then be displayed in rotation at other sites that have also signed up for the exchange program, and you agree to save space on your site to display other banners within the exchange.

There are, however, a few drawbacks with these programs. First, your ad will only be shown once for every two times that a visitor to your site sees a banner from the exchange. Secondly, you may have very limited control over where your banners will appear and, likewise, little say over which banners will appear on your site. (There are, however, a growing number of exchanges that allow you to specify.) Thirdly, many exchanges force participating sites to incorporate a link back to the banner exchange's homepage.

However, as these services are free it may be worth trying one out for a set period of time. Furthermore, many exchanges offer tailored statistics reports. These reports provide information on how often ads have been displayed on your site as well as how often your banner was put up on other sites. This information will help you to measure the exchange's success.

For more information on banner exchanges check out the following resources:

- *Link Exchange (www.linkexchange.com).* The Link Exchange is the most widely used free banner exchange. Set up by the same subsidiary of Microsoft that manages ListBot, the Link Exchange covers a staggering 500,000 sites that collectively reach nearly half of the Web's traffic. As with many other similar exchanges, for every two times that you display a banner on your Web site, you automatically receive a credit that entitles you to have your ad displayed once on another site. Although the degree of control you have over where your banner appears is limited, the Link Exchange provides you with daily reports detailing traffic figures.
- *UK Banners (www.ukbanners.com).* UK Banners is one of the most popular UK-based exchanges. It also works on a much more symmetrical ratio than the majority of other sites. For every 10 times a banner is displayed on your site, your banner ad appears eight times elsewhere within the exchange.
- *Mark Welch's Banner List (www.markwelch.com).* A vast directory of banner exchange programs both in Europe and the US.

Other types of online advertising

A few years ago online advertising was limited to the banner format. Following the decline in banner click-through rates, however, various other types of e-advertising have emerged. Here is an overview of the most common methods.

Advertorials

Advertorials are adverts that are intended to resemble editorial content. They are either incorporated seamlessly into an existing Web site, or they are used as the basis of a completely new site altogether (see 'The Web site as advert' later on in this chapter).

Interstitials

Interstitials are ads that appear on a Web browser as a new page is loading. The obvious advantage they have over banner ads is that while they are on the screen, they are not competing with any other text or graphics for the user's attention. The disadvantage, however, is that they have a tendency to annoy users. As they only appear in between pages they inevitably make download times slower. Furthermore, the emergence of broadband technologies which promise almost instant online access and faster download times could ultimately make the interstitial extinct.

Superstitials

Superstitials are interstitials that only play once a Web page has been completely downloaded. Superstitials tend to be larger than interstitials (virtually taking over the full screen) and have higher production values. The reason for this is that they need to be so attractive that the net user will wait for 30 seconds or so before clicking off the superstitial to see the already downloaded Web page behind. Due to their slick use of audio and video they tend to be expensive to produce. Feedback from companies that have pioneered the use of superstitials has, however, been overwhelmingly positive. Nike, for instance, claims that its superstitial campaign generated far more Web traffic than any of its previous banner-based campaigns.

Sponsorships

The Internet market research company eMarketer has predicted that an increasing number of companies will plump for sponsorships in place of banner ad campaigns over the next few years.

Online sponsorships, typically, are partnerships between a commercial Web site and an information-based Web resource. Through sponsorship, companies can become more closely associated with a site than they can via other methods such as banner placements. The costs involved, however, tend to be a lot higher. As well as Web sites, it is also possible to sponsor discussion groups and electronic newsletters.

To give you some idea of how popular each e-advertising method is, here are some percentages related to online ad spending issued in a report from the Internet Advertising Bureau in 2000:

Banner ads	59%
Sponsorships	28%
Inter/Superstitials	4%
E-mail	1%
Other	8%

It is important to remember that the above figures are based on advertising *budgets* alone. Therefore, while there are a lot more e-mail ads out there than interstitial or superstitials, e-mail-based advertising is a lot cheaper to produce.

E-mail advertising

E-mail advertising offers companies with a limited marketing budget a cost-effective means of targeting potential customers. E-mail advertising differs from spam (junk e-mail) in that it is incorporated within messages that are sent to willing subscribers. There are two main forms of e-mail-based ads: newsletter ads and subscriber lists.

Newsletter ads are ads that are included within subscription-based newsletters. If you spot a newsletter which holds an obvious appeal for your target audience and which has an impressive number of subscribers, it could be worth making some enquiries. These ads are either in a plain text 'advertorial' format, or (in HTML-based newsletters) they will be banner ads.

Subscriber lists are lists of people who have subscribed to receive adverts. The main reason people sign up for these lists is because they are given incentives (entry into a free prize draw, for instance). This means that a lot of people receiving these e-mail ads have no interest whatsoever in their content.

For more information on e-mail advertising visit the direct e-mail list source at Copywriter (www.copywriter.com). This provides a list of companies with subscription-based e-mail lists, e-newsletters that carry ads, and even newsgroups that can be sponsored.

Planning an e-advertising campaign

If anything, careful planning is more important with online advertising than it is offline. Every stage of the campaign must be thought through in order to eliminate the risk of misdirecting your ads towards inappropriate audiences. The structure of your advertising campaign should therefore follow the 10 steps outlined below:

1. Set realistic and measurable objectives.
2. Work out your budget.
3. Clarify who your ad is intended for.
4. Research the online media these people are likely to visit.
5. Develop an advertising schedule (incorporating timescales, media targets and so on).
6. Design the ad(s).
7. Send the ad(s) to relevant publishers (the sites you are going to advertise on).
8. Track the response.
9. Analyse the results.
10. Review and refine your advertising strategy.

Obviously, if you are willing and able to use an external e-marketing agency to help you design and place your online ads, then you will be able to bypass some of the above steps. Even if you do outsource, however, it is important that you monitor the campaign's progress at regular intervals and don't rely solely on the opinion of the company whose services you are paying for.

Buying online advertising space

Although there are many specialist agencies that can help you plan online advertising campaigns, buying advertising space on the Internet is not difficult. When you see a site you want to advertise with, all you need to do is ask for their media pack, find out their rates and ask for a profile of their audience. Generally, advertising rates for banners are worked out in one of three ways: CPM rates, CPA rates and day rates.

CPM rates

CPM stands for cost per thousand page impressions (the M being the Roman numeral for 1000). This remains by far the most widely used pricing model despite the fact that a page impression can mean different things. In terms of banner ads it typically means that the banner is displayed on a page of a site 1000 times. That does not mean, however, that the banner was actually seen 1000 times. For one thing, the person visiting the site may have set their browser not to display banners or, even if they haven't, may not look at or take notice of your ad. Furthermore, the banner may even be placed out of view at the foot of the page ('below the fold' to use net-head terminology).

In terms of e-mail advertising, an 'impression' refers to your ad's inclusion on one e-mail message. So, as with banner ads, 1000 impressions does not necessarily mean 1000 people have seen the ad (or even the message it appeared in). Indeed, a lot of recipients will simply delete the message without even opening it. This will still count as an impression.

CPA rates

Cost per action rates are more accurate than CPM measurements because they are based only on an Internet user's response to your ad. According to this more sophisticated pricing model, you pay only for each time someone clicks through a banner to link to your Web site. Although this system is clearly more attractive for advertisers, you may only be offered this price model if you have advertised previously on the Web site.

Day rates

The oldest and most straightforward form of advertising rate is the day rate method. This is where your banner is put up on a Web site for a set fee for a certain period of time. This is often the model used for when ads are placed in conjunction with some descriptive 'advertorial' copy. For instance, Yahoo!'s Web launch page (which spotlights new Web sites) allows companies to pay for a slot within the section. Each entry is typically made up of a site screen shot, a short site description (written by the advertiser) as well as a banner ad. This service costs US$1000 (or £650) for a one-week placement, although Yahoo! guarantees that over 150,000 people will see each 'listing'.

Before spending money on ad space online you should have the following questions in mind:

- Which rate method is being used?
- How much is the rate?
- Is this rate negotiable? (It often is, especially on smaller sites.)
- What is the audience profile?
- What are the criteria for the ad (dimension, deadlines, etc)?
- How will results be measured (will the publisher report activity)?
- What is the payment schedule?

Where to advertise

It goes without saying that the more targeted your online advertising campaign is, the better the results will be. If your banners are seen only by people who fall within the perimeter of your target audience then you will be guaranteed greater value for money than if they are seen by a general cross-section of net users.

You therefore need to think very carefully about the sites your target audience already visits. These may include competitor's sites, e-zines or online journals relating to your industry, or relevant consumer interest sites. When you are researching where to advertise you could start by looking at where your immediate competitors place their banners. You could also contact companies that advertise on sites you are interested in and ask how effective they have found their banners to be. One of the most popular methods of targeting banner ads to their appropriate audience is to buy advertising space on a search engine based on keywords, so that your banner will be shown every time a user types in a keyword relating to your site. This means you have to tell the search engine which keywords you want your banner to appear under (these can be the same words you use in your meta-tags). Although this type of 'keyword linking' can be up to twice as expensive as a non-specified CPM rate, the results are often over twice as effective. Furthermore, some search engines (such as Yahoo!, Excite and Alta Vista) also allow you to target regions or demographic groups.

Another reason search engines prove effective for advertisers is that they are never final destinations in themselves. As Jerry Yang, the co-founder of Yahoo! remarked, 'People only visit us on the way to somewhere else.' In other words, people arrive at a search engine with the intention of linking to other sites, whether via listings (free or paid for) or banners. However, it is not just search engines that can provide such a tailored and targeted approach. Amazon and other large online retailers can place ads that relate to the type of product a visitor is looking for. As Simon Collin has observed, 'This type of predictive modelling can improve click-through rates up to 10 per cent.'

Advertising placement services

There are various Internet-based services that can assist you in formulating your advertising campaign, although most of them come with a hefty price tag attached. If, however, saving time is more of a priority than saving money, and if you would rather your e-advertising efforts were coordinated by experienced professionals with access to the most up-to-date Internet technologies, then placement services are worth looking into. Here are some of the most popular services on the Web:

- *Double Click (www.doubleclick.net)*. DoubleClick has attracted a string of high-profile international clients, due to its insistence on CPA (cost per action) rates. The company uses its wide network of sites to place banner advertising that companies only pay for if and when a user acts upon (that is, clicks through) the banner.
- *Adventure Network (www.ad-venture.com)*. This New York based service provides advertisers with 'targeting by site, affinity group, and network'.
- *Flycast (www.flycast.com)*. Flycast enables companies to conduct local online advertising as it uses tracking software that can discover the geographic location of a user's computer.

- *2CanMedia (www.2canmedia.com)*. 2CanMedia provides advertisers with a site-matching service aimed at creating 'synergy' between publishers and advertisers.
- *Ad Hunter (www.adhunter.co.uk)*. This UK-based service offers a cheaper alternative to other media placement services mentioned here. It provides access to a wide range of offline and online classified advertising throughout the UK.

The Web site as advert

As the Internet progresses, the overlap between advertising and content becomes even greater, as commercial interests are increasingly being served by meeting the requirements of the end user. In 1995 (the first year of the banner ad) advertising and information were easily distinguishable, but now as useful information is seen as the key to winning over new customers, informative Web sites are being used as in-depth, interactive adverts. Indeed, advertising companies are increasingly using Web sites as the main focus of an ad campaign. Rather than simply placing loads of banners everywhere, many advertisers prefer to view the Web site itself as the ultimate advert for a product or company. Kevin Roberts, CEO for Saatchi and Saatchi US, recently told me that Web sites are preferable to offline advertising methods because they enable companies to 'connect' with their customers at a deeper level than ever before. However, the problem in viewing a Web site as an advert is that it can often stifle the interaction between the company and its customers.

The paradox of ad sites, and e-advertising in general, is that the less like an advert the site is, the more effectively it will advertise what you have to offer. Advertisers who are willing to use the Web site as a means of involving visitors in the site's message (through chat rooms, bulletin boards and so on) are clearly going to have the advantage.

Advertising on your site

If you decide to seek advertising on someone else's site you may also decide to sell advertising space on your own site. Indeed, selling ad space may provide you with the funds needed to spend money on advertising elsewhere. If the content of your site holds obvious appeal for potential advertisers, e-advertising can be a way of increasing your revenue stream, of building relationships with other sites, and of adding value to your site. Below are some guidelines to follow if you are interested in attracting potential advertisers.

Keep rates simple

The most straightforward rate systems (at least from an ad publisher's perspective) are worked out on day or week rates. This means you don't have to worry about tracking click-through or page impressions, as you would if you used CPM or CPA rates.

Prove your popularity

If you are working with a rate system based on duration, you will need to prove, with as much accuracy as possible, how popular your site is with the advertiser's target audience. Fortunately, most Web hosting services are able to provide reasonably accurate traffic figures.

To allay advertisers' doubts, however, it may be worthwhile to download free tracking software that can provide a more detailed visitor profile. For instance, the tracking software available from Extreme Tracking (www.extremetracking.com) can provide information not only on how many people are visiting your site but also on how those people get there (search engines, links from other sites, e-mails and so on). It even tells you what keywords a visitor has typed in on a search engine to reach your site.

Find willing advertisers

Your aim should be to find not one, but a number of companies willing to advertise on your site. This will enable you to rotate ads on a weekly basis so that you will never have empty or unpaid-for banner space. Ultimately, you should also try and set up an automated payment procedure whereby your company bills clients' accounts once a month and displays their banners on an ongoing basis.

Add a directory to your site

If you set up a useful directory of Web sites relevant to your industry at your site, it is likely that potential advertisers will start approaching *you*. Furthermore, approaching other companies about being included in your paid-for directory is a lot more likely to generate a positive response than if you are asking companies if they would like a banner on your site.

Summary

Online advertising can help both large and small organizations fulfil their marketing objectives. For the big players it is a vital way of building brand recognition, while for small to medium-sized companies it can help both to direct traffic to a site and convert that traffic into sales.

As Internet users are becoming more cynical about banner ads, new online advertising methods are emerging that are proving successful in satisfying the needs of both advertiser and customer. This is because advertisers are starting to come to terms with the fact that the Internet is a 'pull' rather than 'push' technology – Internet users pull material towards them, rather than having messages pushed upon them. The challenge for advertisers is therefore to ensure their messages are *chosen* by their target audiences. As more and more lateral approaches are being deployed in the form of advertorials, sponsorships, newsletter ads and so on, many companies are already proving that this is a challenge advertisers can rise to with confidence.

twelve

E-publicity

To help your site create an impression in the minds of your target customers, you will need to think of ways to boost its publicity, or PR (public relations), value. This means you will have to build up reciprocal relationships with the online and offline media by providing journalists with newsworthy information about your site or company.

Of course, as we have explored elsewhere in the book, by building a Web site your company has already become part of the media. In theory, the Internet means you can get your message across without relying on intermediaries such as journalists, editors, publishers and producers. In practice, however, brand awareness depends on strong and mutually beneficial media relations. After all, people are always more likely to believe what someone else says about you, than what you say about yourself.

Furthermore, PR is a highly cost-effective form of promotion when compared to advertising. Not only is editorial coverage free, but its value increases because it hasn't been paid for. Although it remains questionable whether the effectiveness of advertising can be accurately measured against that of public relations, when people have attempted to do so they have found that editorial has about three times the impact of an ad within the same publication. It is certainly the case that, by and large, people buy a newspaper for its news content not for the adverts, no matter how attractive they are.

The purpose of this chapter is to provide an overview of the Internet as a tool for effective media relations that will help increase and consolidate your Web site's online and offline profile.

Making news

Although the Internet remains a hot media topic, ever more effort is required on the part of e-marketers to find a newsworthy angle.

Back in the mid-1990s, when the Web was first being used for commercial purposes, it was enough simply to announce that you had a Web site – it was a rare event.

A lot has changed in cyberspace since then. Now it is assumed that every business of note has an online presence. In fact, it would be easier for a major company to gain press coverage by announcing it *didn't* have a Web site. To ensure your Web site catches the imagination of relevant journalists and editors, it needs to provide something of real value to them. This means, as with other e-marketing activity, you need to adopt an outside-in approach; in other words, think about what interests publications and their readers, *then* think about the message you want to get across. Gaining media coverage is all about finding the middle ground between the aims of a publication and your company.

Below are some of the most effective ways to bring out your Web site's full publicity potential.

Court controversy

Taking a controversial stance on an issue of topical news interest is one of the quickest routes towards media coverage. Think of the press attention gained by Web sites that use controversial MP3 technology (which helps users swap free music files with each other). You need to make sure, however, that the statements you make won't end up alienating your target audience.

Find the 'man bites dog' angle

There is an old media truism that states, 'If a dog bites a man it is not news, but if a man bites a dog it probably is.' If you can find a way to turn the status quo upside down, then you will be well on the way to media attention.

The human factor

People would rather read about other people than about technology. When putting together a story that relates to your Web site, always try to add a human slant.

Produce new findings

One of the ways to guarantee media coverage is to conduct a survey and report the findings. The Internet provides you with a cost-effective means of contacting groups of people en masse, either via e-mail or through your Web site. If you can provide a new and intriguing insight into how and why people are using the Internet, your media release will be viewed as a welcome addition to an editor's e-mail box.

Durex, for instance, published research findings that showed that among Internet users, buying Durex products online is preferable to the embarrassment occasionally suffered in the real world. Of course, the tabloid editors' imagination ran riot and Durex achieved maximum press exposure. The success of this story is not only attributable to the fact that it has wide public appeal, but it is also due to its direct relevance to the brand in question.

Be first

If your site is the first to do something it may have a right to be taken seriously as a news story. The Pizza Hut site received the most media coverage it had experienced when it was announced that it would be the first to offer a pizza delivery service via the Internet.

Follow up

If you find a story that relates to your site, follow it up by sending a tailored press release to the appropriate editor. Most publications like to provide follow-up pieces, as it creates consistency between different issues.

Find a topical angle

Finding a topical angle for your Web site will help you to build media relationships. After all, if you can provide a love story for Valentine's day, a Santa story for Christmas and a chocolate egg story for Easter, you are likely to win favour with editors.

Set up an awards scheme

Once you have a substantial amount of traffic at your Web site you could set up an awards programme relevant to your industry. When the results come through, you can then contact the winner and arrange for a member of your staff and a photographer to go and present the award. A photograph of a well-known industry figure holding up an award with your logo on it is worth its weight in gold as part of an electronic press pack.

Hold a competition

Running a competition in conjunction with a magazine, newspaper or e-zine is another effective means of gaining media coverage, provided the prizes are appealing to the publication's readership. You are even more likely to gain coverage if you throw in a few freebies for the journalists themselves.

The main advantage of holding a competition via the media is that you can almost guarantee that any coverage you receive will be glowing. This is because it is in the publication's best interest to boost the value of the competition prizes they are giving away to readers.

Media research

Before you decide *how* you are going to present your story, you need to find out *who* it is aimed at. To do this you will need to undertake some media research and work out which publications are likely to be interested. Every time you come across a journalist who would be likely to cover your Web site, find out their contact details and add them to your e-mail media list. Things to look out for include:

- *Competitor coverage.* Look out for journalists who have written about your competitors, as they may be equally interested in your company or Web site.
- *Related issues.* Publications that cover issues relating to your site should, of course, be a prime target.
- *Site listings.* Magazines and newspapers often set aside space for listings and reviews of different Web sites.

- *Trade titles.* Trade publications relating to your industry are likely to be receptive to any useful information you send.
- *Audience interest.* Look for media that are relevant to the interests of your various target audiences. After all, there is no point in being mentioned in the media if no one interested in what your site offers will see it.

As it is impossible to watch, read and interact with all the media that could be relevant to your site, you will have to take a few short-cuts. For online media, the search engines provide an obvious starting point as they enable you to filter out irrelevant sites by using industry-specific keywords. There are also vast numbers of online media directories that incorporate traditional media alongside Web sites and e-zines. Here's a selection of some of the most user-friendly Web-based media directories:

- *Media Finder (www.mediafinder.com).* Media Finder provides a comprehensive database of international publications, with a variety of search options.
- *Brad (www.brad.co.uk).* Brad provides full listings for national and local media, including both the business and consumer press. As with the print version, however, Brad online is a paid-for service. Prices vary according to your media requirements.
- *Media UK (www.mediauk.com).* This UK-based directory offers free and fee-based listings (see Figure 12.1).
- *New Jour (gort.ucsd.edu/newjour/NewJourWel).* Arguably the most comprehensive e-media directory, New Jour indexes Web sites, new and archived newsletters, e-zines and journals, many of which are not listed anywhere else. Its user-friendly search facility enables you to search by alphabetical category or keyword.

A full index of all the online media directories can be found at the Yahoo! site (dir.yahoo.com/News_and_Media/WebDirectories).

Handling journalists the right way

Journalists require easy access to organized, relevant, credible and topical information. To build up a relationship with a journalist you need to understand this, and be prepared to give him or her what they want. Although journalists may be some of the hardest people

Figure 12.1 Media UK Web site. Media UK is one the leading online media directories

to win over, it is worth the effort. After all, a glowing piece of editorial on your company will always prove more effective than placing an advert in the same publication. Below are some general tips to follow in order to get on (and stay on) the right side of the press.

Identify their requirements

All journalists have their own specific requirements relating not only to the type of information they receive, but also *how* they receive it. Some journalists still prefer traditional means of communication (phone, fax or post) to e-mail. Even among those who do prefer corresponding via e-mail, they may still have certain requirements you need to consider. For instance, some will want lengthy information (media releases and so on) to be incorporated within the body of an e-mail while others will prefer you to send it as an attached file. Even if they are completely unfussy, it always makes a good impression to ask.

Target your correspondence

In an ideal world, no two media releases would look the same and
every journalist would receive information that had been tailored to
his or her specific interests and writing style. In reality, however,
this is not always a practical option. Even though you may not be
able to personalize each correspondence to every individual journalist, you should try and differentiate between the various *types* of
journalist. There are business reporters, feature writers, financial
columnists, technology journalists and so on, all with very different
concerns. Never distribute press releases *en masse* as if every journalist were exactly the same.

Be informative

Although providing unbiased and relevant information is always
important on the Internet, it is even more crucial when dealing with
journalists. If you can provide valuable insights into the direction
your industry or market is heading you will be forever valued by
the media (see 'Becoming a media resource').

Provide ease of access

Due to the tight deadlines they work to, journalists want instant
and convenient access to information. Not only should you provide
a user-friendly media centre at your site, but you should also make
sure that e-mails sent by editors and journalists are responded to
within a matter of hours.

Provide facts

When it comes to media releases, journalists want hard facts rather
than subjective opinion. Dates, financial figures, names, your Web
site address, statistics and research findings are therefore all
welcome additions to your media release. By the same token, an
abundance of adjectives and unproven superlatives ('best ever',
'amazing', 'most successful' and so on) should be resisted.

Adhere to deadline dates

Contacting a journalist on deadline day is the ultimate PR *faux pas*. Any obstacle put in the path of editors and journalists in their attempt to get everything completed on time will be very unwelcome, to say the least. The best time to make contact is actually on the day of publication itself, when the manic frenzy of deadline day is over. Of course, if you are contacting an online publication there may not be one deadline day, as its content is probably refreshed all the time. In this case it doesn't matter when you approach them (although Monday mornings and Friday afternoons are best avoided).

The e-media release

Whether you are targeting online or offline media, sending releases via the Internet offers certain advantages over the traditional format. As well as being more convenient and cost-effective, it also enables a degree of interactivity that is impossible with traditional, static releases.

Style and content

Although the subject matter of media releases should stay the same whether they are in print or electronic format, there are some differences in terms of how you write and lay out a release for the Internet. Below are some guidelines to observe when writing and sending releases in e-mail format.

Keep it short

Although the length of press releases has traditionally been between 300 and 400 words, this is too long for an e-mail format, when readers have to scroll down to read the text. Limit the length of your e-mail releases to around the 150-word mark.

Condense relevant information at the top of the release

E-media releases should include a very short (one or two sentence) paragraph at the top of the screen that summarizes the content of the release. As Business Week's marketing reporter Ellen Newborne comments, 'Journalists hate having to scroll past contact information and the obligatory description just to get to the subject of the release.'

Keep company descriptions brief

Journalists already suffering from information overload have little time for reading lengthy company descriptions from a computer screen. Five or six words are plenty to provide a brief overview of what your company or Web site does.

Think of the 'elevator pitch'

Silicon Valley entrepreneurs talk of the 'elevator pitch' as the 30-second straight-to-the-point pitch to get VCs (Venture Capitalists) interested in their big idea. When writing your electronic releases, imagine you are telling what it is you have to say in a 30-second elevator ride. This should produce the succinct and informal style that suits the e-mail format.

Provide links

Print media releases only contain as much information as the space (normally two sheets) allows. With electronic media releases however, you can provide links to more in-depth information throughout the release. Links to your Web site should certainly be incorporated within each release, as well as links to the e-mail addresses of each media contact.

Avoid over-formality

When sending printed press releases, there are certain rules you must conform to. For instance, the words 'MEDIA RELEASE' and

'ENDS' must always appear at the top and bottom of the release, respectively. Such formalities are not necessary when sending releases via e-mail, as they can often prove counter-productive. E-mail is essentially an immediate and informal medium, and this fact should be acknowledged when writing and sending releases.

As well as the obvious differences mentioned above, some elements of writing media releases remain the same regardless of the format. Here are some guidelines that apply equally to releases sent via fax, post or e-mail:

- *Short headlines.* Your headline should summarize the subject of the release in as few words as possible (preferably in fewer than six).
- *Answer the 'w' questions.* All media releases should answer five basic questions: Who? What? Where? When? Why? Furthermore, these questions should, where possible, be addressed in the first couple of paragraphs.
- *Include quotes.* Quotes liven up media releases by adding a human element to the story. Make sure any quotes you include are genuine, however. Journalists have an uncanny knack of sniffing out quotes that are fabricated by PR people who couldn't be bothered to source a genuine comment.
- *Incorporate third-party opinion.* Incorporating comments from third parties will add to the value of your release, as it will lend more authority to what you have to say. It will always be preferable to have an industry pundit endorse your Web site, rather than to have someone within your company say how great it is. You could even include customer testimonials within your release (provided they are authentic, of course).
- *Don't expect instant results.* Although it may be worthwhile to send out a media release when you have launched or relaunched your site, it probably won't result in media coverage. All it will do is get your name in circulation, so that the next time you distribute a release journalists will actually know who you are. While the Internet is a fast moving medium, strong media relationships will always take time to build up.
- *Check before you send.* The other piece of advice that should always be adhered to is to make sure you proof read releases thoroughly before they are sent out. Spelling and grammatical errors, ambiguous statements, repetition and any inaccurate information must be rectified before the release arrives in a journalist or editor's e-mail box.

Distributing e-media releases

Once you have compiled a comprehensive list of editors and journalists' e-mail addresses, distributing releases is relatively easy. Ideally, each release should be accompanied with a brief e-mail message tailored to the individual recipient. However, when you are sending a release out to hundreds of journalists simultaneously, this is not a practical option. When distributing releases *en masse* you should make use of the Bcc: (blind carbon copy) e-mail box, rather than the To: or Cc: options, if you want to avoid letting each journalist know all the other journalists the release has been sent to. By cutting and pasting all the addresses from your mailing list document into the Bcc: box you can ensure they remain invisible.

Another way to distribute your e-media releases is to use an online news wire service. News wire services feed the online and offline media with virtually every kind of story imaginable. They are particularly popular among business publications, as they provide the most comprehensive and up-to-date resource available for the business reporter. Although you have to pay a nominal fee to have your release distributed via these services, it can prove extremely worthwhile. It is a way of reaching a lot of journalists in a very short time and, as the journalists are pulling the information towards them (by opting into each service) it is a safer, spam-free alternative to distributing them yourself. There are many online services, both for Europe and the US, but there is no general consensus of opinion as to which is the best: it all depends on the nature of your site and its target audience. Ultimately, however, it doesn't really matter which service you choose to use as there is a substantial amount of shared information between the services, with releases duplicated on different sites.

The two main international services are: Business Wire (www. businesswire.com) and PR Newswire (www.prnewswire.com). To use either of these services, follow these simple steps:

- Visit their site.
- Set up an account.
- Put your release together.
- Send the release via e-mail to the site.
- Confer with the account executive (via phone or e-mail) over which editors and journalists should receive the release and when.

■ Wait for a confirmation e-mail to say the release has been distributed.

Electronic press packs

Press packs are used to provide members of the media with a general overview of your company or Web site. They typically include a contact list, recent media releases, a company profile or backgrounder and mini CVs for key staff members. Effective press packs provide journalists with an insight into the past, present and predicted future of a business.

The advantage of online press packs is that they can be updated and distributed at minimal cost, and can include various interactive elements such as links to your Web site. Your online press pack should provide as much information as necessary for general media enquiries, and should also make clear that more detailed information can be found at your site.

E-mail pitches

Another way of contacting editors and journalists is to send an e-mail proposing an article. The advantage of this approach is that it can be more informal and less assumptive than sending out releases. As pitches must be targeted with the interests of each individual journalist in mind they are also more likely to solicit a response (even if that response later proves unfruitful).

E-mail pitches take two basic forms. You can either e-mail a journalist proposing that *he or she* writes an article on your company or, if you feel up to it, you can e-mail an editor and propose that *you* write an article.

Contributing an article on your business area or a subject relating to your Web site, with your name and Web site address at the bottom, can prove beneficial to both you and the publication. For the publication, it means it can get the authoritative opinion of an industry insider; for you it means exposure and the endorsement an editorial piece provides. As a result it can help build your status as an authority in your business sector.

If you are suggesting an article, make it clear who you are in the first sentence, and explain why you think the article would be suitable for the publication's audience. Web site and e-zine editors in particular are likely to welcome e-mail pitches due to the fast moving nature of their publications. To increase the likelihood of positive responses you could offer to promote the publication on your Web site (via a link, or free banner for instance).

Here's an authentic example of an e-mail pitch that received a positive response:

Hi Sara,

I am a Partner at a London based law firm which handles a lot of high profile dot com related cases. I am writing to propose a feature on how Internet start-ups can avoid the various legal pitfalls that can be encountered by Web sites. As a regular reader of your publication, I feel this would not only be of interest to your readership, but would also fit the authoritative tone of your magazine. I believe it would be perfect for your monthly 'Top Ten Tips…' section. Although it will provide solid and practical advice, I will refrain from legal jargon and write in a lively and accessible style. The word count and timescale are flexible.

Let me know what you think.

Regards,
Jamie Gibson

By taking the effort to tailor and personalize each e-mail pitch message, you are twice as likely (if not more) to gain a reply. Although this may seem a rather time-consuming option, it is better to receive responses from 10 personalized messages than to receive none from 100 identical pitches.

Becoming a media resource

To achieve ongoing publicity for a Web site it is necessary to build mutually beneficial relationships between the site and the media. One of the best ways to do this is to turn a section of your site into a media centre. This will involve providing journalists with relevant contact details and information, such as a media release archive.

If you really want to win favour with the press you could also provide inside information on your industry in general, as well as your company. Indeed, some companies incorporate unedited material from competitors on their site. This unfiltered approach may seem to go against the grain of traditional PR practice but, perhaps for that very reason, it is welcome by journalists and editors. If you can establish yourself as an authoritative and objective source of information on your industry, you are far more likely to be listened to when you are telling journalists about your company. Don't forget, every day of their working lives journalists are bombarded with media releases that are full of self-praise but little else. By aiming to be the source, as well as the subject, of media interest, you will be able to build two-way media relationships and long-term publicity opportunities.

Here are some guidelines for creating a user-friendly media centre on your site:

- *Categorize information.* Don't just provide a list of press releases in reverse chronological order: categorize information around themes, products and services. Journalists can rarely be bothered to trawl through screen after screen of information, unless it is made explicit how the information could be useful to them.
- *Make the location obvious.* As soon as a journalist arrives at your site, he or she needs to be guided to the press area as quickly as possible.
- *Add a search engine facility.* A search engine is always a welcome addition to any online press area.
- *Include press articles.* Press articles about your company will help provide journalists with a media context and they will also be of interest to your wider audience of site visitors.
- *Provide an e-mail update option.* Journalists won't always be willing or able to return to your site, so provide them with the option of receiving update messages every time something significant is added to the centre.
- *Add links to your site.* Providing links to related sites (including those of your immediate competitors) will provide another incentive for journalists to visit.
- *Incorporate financial information.* Companies that keep an open account book are going to be valued by the media and public alike as a trustworthy business with nothing to hide.
- *Keep nothing back.* The media will be most likely to turn to your site when you are the subject of negative publicity. Making sure that in times of potential crisis, unfiltered information is provided, means journalists will be more likely to present your side

of the story. As Lord Northcliffe (founder of the *Daily Mail*) famously put it: 'News is what somebody somewhere wants to suppress, all the rest is advertising.' By suppressing potentially damaging information, companies only succeed in increasing its media value.

Provide contact information. If a journalist is interested in a story he or she will need to know who to contact. As well as making sure every piece of information in the media centre incorporates the relevant contact details, you could also provide an electronic media hotline.

For more inspiration it is worth taking a look at sites that already run successful media areas. These include:

Napster (www.napster.com). As Napster's file-swapping service was rarely out of the headlines, it is no surprise to find that it had a large press centre rich with content (see Figure 12.2). This

Figure 12.2 Napster Web site. The controversial and ill-fated Napster site included an exceptional press area

included links to media articles, company backgrounds, FAQ sheets, press conference details and various other press announcements.

- *Lycos (www.lycos.com – .co.uk)*. The Lycos press area is integrated within the main site and very easy for the first-time visitor to find. It prides itself on having an 'open book' policy and offers unfiltered information on just about every aspect of the company.
- *Slice (www.slice.co.uk)*. The UK-based PR company, Slice, offers a very user-friendly press area. The search facility is particularly effective.
- *Gateway (www.gateway.com)*. As well as providing a mine of information on the company, Gateway's press area also provides live webcasts of events, speeches and conferences.
- *Excite (www.excite.com)*. Alongside contact details and a media hotline, the Excite press centre also provides a downloadable media kit.

Guerrilla marketing

The term 'guerrilla marketing' refers to any extreme or outlandish attempt to generate publicity, either online or offline. The logic behind guerrilla marketing is simple: if a company promotes itself in a unique fashion it will not only be able to gain press coverage, but will also stick in people's minds and encourage word-of-mouth publicity. Many people equate guerrilla marketing with gimmicky publicity stunts, but there can be a lot more to it than that.

Companies can use guerrilla marketing tactics not only to draw attention to themselves, but also to help create a fresh and distinctive identity. For this reason guerrilla marketing is especially popular among e-marketers as a means of drawing attention to a Web site. Yahoo! is one Internet company that swears by the guerrilla method. For instance, the company took part in an event called Cow Parade in which cows were decorated according to different themes. Yahoo!'s 'udderly moovelous' (as it put in a release) pair of purple plastic cows were installed with an Internet facility that enabled members of the crowd to send 'moomail' messages to each other. Although this tactic was undeniably off the wall, it worked because it maintained a degree of relevance to the service it was promoting (Yahoo! mail). Guerrilla marketing can therefore be worthwhile, but only if it remains consistent with your other marketing activity.

Online press conferences

If you have a major announcement to make that will be considered significant by various key members of the media, it could be worthwhile holding an online press conference. These are a particularly good way of handling negative publicity (see below), as they provide you with the ultimate chance to set the record straight. The other advantages of holding a press conference via the Internet include:

- *Convenience*. It is more convenient for busy journalists and editors to take part in an online conference than to attend one in the real world.
- *International participation*. If you have built up relationships with the international media, online press conferences enable foreign journalists to participate without buying a plane ticket.
- *Open access*. Customers, industry pundits, investors and other audiences can also take part.
- *No notebooks*. As everyone who takes part in the conference can print a transcript of the entire event, there is no need for note-taking.
- *Unlimited attendance*. Whereas in a traditional press conference the number of participants is restricted by the size of the venue, at online conferences attendance is unlimited.

To host a press conference on the Internet, you will need to set up a conference chat system. This involves installing special conference/chat software such as E-ware (www.eware.com), I-chat (www.ichat.com) or Proxicom (www.proxicom.com). When the software is installed, you can conduct a conference at any time. To ensure a satisfactory attendance rate you should e-mail journalists well in advance, announcing the conference, and then send another e-mail message the day before. Make sure you specify the subject, as well as the time and date of the conference in your e-mail messages.

PR is everything

While in the real world PR is all too often seen as a secondary supplement to a company's marketing strategy, on the Internet PR is everything.

Offline, a business is always distanced from the media, trying to influence it from the sidelines and hoping for the best. On the Internet, however, a business is a part of, not apart from, the media. As a result, every e-business activity falls under the PR umbrella as everything uploaded onto the Web or sent via e-mail holds the potential to affect public relations.

Internet PR is, in many ways, more straightforward than public relations in the real world. Instead of communicating messages via an intermediary, such as a journalist, information can be presented directly. Having a voice is no longer a problem: the challenge lies in making sure that voice is heard. The net is a customer-pull medium, so to succeed at public relations on the Internet, it is important to adopt an 'outside-in' approach and think from the net users' perspective.

Negative publicity

As the democratic nature of the Internet enables anyone to have a voice, the truth is always out there. This means people with a complaint against a company can share their grievance with thousands of others in a consumer discussion group. In severe cases they can even vent their disdain by setting up 'anti-sites' such as Microsucks.com or Britishscareways (www.aviation-uk.com). The more companies try to spin the Web, the more they risk getting tangled in a mess of their own making. Not only do the web and Usenet discussion groups need to be monitored, but also companies need to incorporate any dissident voices into their own e-activity. Web site forums, message boards, chat rooms and other interactive facilities can aid the inclusion of the audience into the message, and therefore limit the potential for negative online publicity.

Companies only become vulnerable on the Internet if the consumer is denied access to their development. If, however, conversation between the business and its market is positively encouraged through bulletin boards, e-mail correspondence, e-surveys and so on the Internet is actually an advantage. As well as large multinationals such as P&G, smaller UK-based companies such as the successful online retailer The Organic Shop (www.theorganicshop.co.uk) are thriving on the Web because they are learning to brand themselves from the 'outside in'. The site evolves in line with the needs of the consumer.

Below are some ways to avoid a publicity crisis.

Compile a media e-mail list

Putting together a list of relevant journalists' e-mail addresses can ensure that, should a crisis situation occur, you can make immediate, simultaneous contact with the press. This will enable you to put across your side of the story before anyone else gets a chance. However, whenever you do contact journalists *en masse,* make sure you put all their e-mail addresses in the Bcc: (blind carbon copy) box. If you put them in the Cc: or To: boxes everyone on the list will see who else you've sent the message to.

You could also include a media centre on your site; see 'Becoming a media resource', above.

Don't cheat the search engines

Locked within the HTML code of every Web site is the meta-tag where Web designers can list keywords to help control how the page is indexed on search engines. There are some rogue designers out there who misuse the meta-tag in order to make their site more attractive to a search engine. Words that they know are frequently typed in to search engines will be inserted into the meta-tag even though they are not relevant to the site. This is the cyberspace equivalent of genetic engineering, and can seriously damage a site's healthy reputation.

Involve third parties

The advantage of online marketing over its real world counterpart is the fact that media coverage doesn't have to depend on third parties. This is also a disadvantage. Without third parties how can the company message be effectively validated? The short answer is it can't. This does not mean it is necessary to shell out for high-profile celebrity endorsement. As many failing dot coms can testify, having the likes of Joanna Lumley or William Shatner endorse a Web site does not automatically result in significantly higher hit counts. What Web users want, by and large, is access to objective information. If the content of a Web site is put together from within the company walls, net surfers will be able to detect bias. If, on the other hand, unpaid third parties are involved, visitors to the site are likely to be considerably less sceptical.

Tell people what they want to know

The Internet enables a company to communicate with all its various audiences, be they customers, investors, journalists, competitors, industry pundits or employees. If the audiences want to find the low-down on the company, they will increasingly be making the Internet their first port of call. However, they only want to hear it from the horse's mouth if the horse is speaking their language.

Provide your staff with media training

Every member of your company should be told how to respond to the media in the event of any enquiries. The Internet's interactive nature makes it the perfect medium for staff training.

Monitor newsgroups

Disgruntled customers or rivals can use newsgroups to share their complaints with the online community. As well as big companies such as Intel, McDonalds, Shell and Microsoft, many small companies have suffered as a result of negative word-of-mouth publicity that was left to breed online. Although it may not seem that harmful to have an attack on your company posted in a discussion group of, say 100 members, the consequences can be far reaching. For instance, a story about Intel's flawed Pentium chip that started in a tiny academic newsgroup ended up on the covers of the *Financial Times* and *The Wall Street Journal* simultaneously.

Investigative journalists are increasingly turning to newsgroups as the first port of call when researching a 'bricks and mortar' or

Internet-based company. Furthermore, consumers use online news-groups to find information about products or services they may want to spend money on. If people are answering their enquiries with recommendations to use your competitors' products or with negative comments about your company, you clearly need to know about it. By monitoring these groups, you will be able to correct misinformation about your Web site and also respond to enquiries with helpful recommendations of your own products.

Searching the newsgroups

As there are hundreds of thousands of Internet-based newsgroups, it would be impossible to visit each one in turn. Instead, you should visit Deja News (www.dejanews.com), which provides a searchable index of all the Usenet newsgroups (Usenet is the most popular system that distributes newsgroups).

Simply type in keywords or phrases relating to your Web site and wait for the Deja search facility to return with not only articles where those words or phrases are found, but also:

- details of the newsgroup in which it was posted;
- the e-mail address of the person who posted it;
- the 'headline' of the message;
- the previous message (where relevant).

This will help you work out which newsgroups you should be concentrating your efforts on, and also will enable you to identify individuals with an interest in (or grievance against) your company or Web site.

Other newsgroup search facilities can be found at:

Newsguy (www.newsguy.com)
Randori (www.randori.com)
Remarq (www.remarq.com)
Liszt (www.liszt.com)
Tile (www.tile.com)

Responding to messages

When you discover comments about your company you will need to judge whether the comments require a response. If the comments are misleading or misinformed then you should certainly attempt to clarify the situation. When dealing with hostile remarks in newsgroups you need to ensure that you don't end up making the situation worse. Equally, if a customer is enquiring about a product or service you offer, you don't want to put them off by using newsgroups as a means of blatant self-promotion. Here are some guidelines to follow when responding to newsgroup articles that affect your business:

- *Be honest*. If people are right to complain, acknowledge this fact before letting them know how you are addressing the problem.
- *Explain who you are*. Unscrupulous companies have been known to mislead newsgroup members by pretending to be other customers. This clear breach of netiquette can result in disaster, however, as newsgroup members have an intuitive ability to spot a commercial message no matter how disguised it is.
- *Avoid jargon*. Technical, business or legal jargon will only confuse people and subsequently cause even more irritation.
- *Respond quickly*. Usenet news and discussion groups are among the fastest moving areas of the Internet. While positive publicity can build up in a short space of time, negative publicity spreads even quicker. Misinformation left unchecked will be taken as fact within about 24 hours.
- *Be conversational*. Write messages in an authentic and human voice. Also, try and keep the dialogue going by asking a question in return.
- *Welcome feedback*. Being thankful for any constructive criticism will form the impression that you are a company more than willing to listen to its customers.
- *Get friendly with newsgroup moderators*. Moderators who are responsible for keeping the discussion on track generally initiate newsgroup topics. By staying on the right side of the moderators, the flow of the discussion is more likely to turn in your favour.

When you have identified the newsgroups that your customers and potential customers participate in, and have built up your status among the group, you can then make regular postings to inform them of new developments. When a negative issue is anticipated, you should post as much pertinent information as possible to relevant newsgroup members and even ask for feedback on how they feel potential future problems can be resolved. This will decrease the chances that disgruntled consumers will provide the press with ammunition for a damning article on your company.

Useful Web sites

There are masses of Web sites that provide advice on publicity and e-media relationships, most originating from the US. Here is a selection of some of the most popular:

- *Marketing Tips (www.marketingtips.com)*. The Marketing Tips site has a particularly useful PR section with advice provided by public relations consultants and marketing reporters. The emphasis is on providing advice for small businesses with an online presence.
- *JV Marketer (www.jvmarketer.com)*. Greg Schliesmann's JV Marketer site enables you to subscribe to a weekly free e-mail newsletter called Breakthrough Internet Marketing. As it centres on cost-effective and free marketing techniques, there is a lot of information on e-media relations. The most useful part, however, is the discussion forum that enables you to ask any question relating to your publicity efforts.
- *Marketing UK (www.marketinguk.co.uk)*. This site provides public relations advice, contact databases, and links to other marketing and publicity sites.
- *PR2 (www.pr2.com)*. The PR2 site offers a free e-mail-based course on how to gain publicity for Web sites. As the home page boldly declares: 'Find out what works and what doesn't, and why you don't need to spend a lot of money to get a whole heap of traffic.'
- *Guerrilla Marketing (www.gmarketing.com)*. Offers information on a wide range of guerrilla marketing tactics.
- *Net B2B (www.netb2b.com)*. The Net B2B site provides PR advice for business-to-business Web sites.
- *Web Site Promotion (www.web-sitepromotion.com)*. This user-friendly site offers a diverse range of tips and techniques for promoting online.

Summary

Your long-term cyberspace survival depends on a good relationship with the online and offline media. Although this does not necessarily cost a lot in terms of money, there is no getting around the fact that it will take a substantial amount of time and effort. Ultimately, good media relationships depend on an honest and objective approach whereby you are willing to concede problems when they arise and accept the existence of your competition.

Just as a lot of e-business success depends on your ability to put yourself in the shoes of your customers, so strong media relationships depend on your willingness to adopt an 'outside-in' approach by understanding the sort of information journalists require. This means being able to support newsworthy happenings by providing unfiltered and comprehensive information. Although this sometimes takes courage, the companies that provide journalists with an open book are the ones that stand to maximize the opportunities for positive coverage, while at the same time limit the potential for negative publicity.

thirteen

Clicks and mortar **marketing**

The dividing line between the Internet and the real world is becoming increasingly blurred. Offline media and communication methods have, at least partially, merged with Internet technology. It is now possible to access the Internet via your mobile phone, a fact that has given rise to a new type of online marketing called m-commerce (or mobile commerce). You can watch TV via the Internet, and log online via the TV. Furthermore, whereas a few years ago there was an evident 'us and them' mentality among both online and offline businesses, there is now a more integrated approach. Traditional 'bricks and mortar' companies are now strengthening their Web presence, while Internet-based operations are spending more of their marketing budgets on building up their offline profile. This chapter looks in more depth at the nature of this offline-online integration, as well as at some of the many ways the real world can help boost your e-marketing activity.

The Internet and the offline media

The interdependent relationship between e-marketing and the offline media is evident in the obvious media interest in the way companies and individuals are using the Internet. Even if you came to the (unwise) conclusion that online audiences are irrelevant to your business, there would be strong arguments for using the Internet as a means of generating offline publicity.

If you can come up with an imaginative angle relating to your Web site you are sure to gain offline media coverage. Most newspapers have Internet or technology sections or supplements and there are many TV and radio shows with net features. There is also a rapidly expanding range of Internet magazines you can target. Many include a 'site of the month' or similar feature, alongside various other references to new or improved Web sites. If by conducting your own research you can shed some light on to the way people like to use the net, or on how online habits are evolving, you will have an advantage over your Web-based competition. Companies that are first to do something online also stand a good chance of gaining press interest.

For instance, when Pizza Hut (www.pizzahut.com) became the first site to enable people to order pizzas online, the coverage it received in the print media around the world reached far more people than it could have done via its Web site alone. The fact that such a recognizable real world business was taking the initiative online ensured substantial media coverage. However, even if your business is not a universally recognized brand name, you can gain offline coverage by making sure your Internet story has a broad 'cross-over' interest (see Chapter 12 for more ideas).

The online/offline media overlap is also evidenced on the Internet itself. Not only do most major TV stations and magazine publishers have a strong Web presence (for instance, BBC TV and IPC Magazines both take the Internet *very* seriously), but also Web sites are incorporating radio and TV elements into their own design. Many companies are creating online radio and TV stations to add value to the users' experience.

Narrowcasting

One of the differences between the online and offline media that is often cited is that whereas traditional media *broad*casts the same message to a mass audience, the Internet *narrow*casts messages to individual and niche audiences. While this argument still holds true, it is evident that various sections of the offline media are developing characteristics more in tune with the Internet. For example, the emergence of digital TV has brought with it a proliferation of channels catering for ever-smaller population segments. Whereas the BBC used to provide only two terrestrial channels catering for a cross-section of the British public, it has now launched various digital channels centering on one theme or subject, such as news or entertainment (BBC News 24 and BBC Choice, respectively). Whether this trend is a direct result of the Internet or not, it means that as well as providing the consumer with more media choice, marketers can now target messages to a greater extent both online *and* offline.

The end of high street shopping?

Although more and more people are starting to shop online it is difficult to see a future where the Internet replaces the real world shopping experience altogether. What seems to be more likely is that online and offline shopping will become integrated to a greater extent. Indeed, companies such as Wal-Mart and Virgin are already combining their Internet and real world activity by incorporating Web consoles into some of their larger stores. This enables customers to visit the company's Web site and order products that are unavailable in the store.

Companies view the Internet not as replacing their real world operations but as a way of supplementing and adding value to them. For instance, a Web site can be used to place orders for products that will then be picked up in person at the store itself. As a Mintel report into UK versus US online shopping concluded, 'rather than heralding the death of the high street, Internet retailing is an alternative channel in a multi-channel future. Traditional retailers feel that it is a basic customer expectation these days and are offering an Internet option as a complement to their existing services'.

Reality sites

As the real world becomes increasingly influenced by the Internet, so the Internet starts to resemble real world environments. Applying familiar real world references to different sections of your site can help put new visitors at ease, and help people get their bearings. For instance The Ministry of Sound Web site includes a VIP room (a registration-based chat room) that clearly evokes the physical setting of the nightclub it promotes.

Furthermore, many sites are starting to use technology to compensate for the customer's inability to see products in a physical setting. Many clothing Web sites provide 360-degree rotational graphics of products and some even provide virtual changing rooms (eg the Diesel site at www.diesel.co.uk; see Figure 13.1). As advanced technologies already exist that will enable touch and smell to be transmitted from a Web site to the user, the Internet's appropriation of real world experience looks set to continue. This ultimately will benefit marketers by aiding the integration of online and offline activity as well as by enriching the entire Internet shopping process.

Integrated advertising

Offline advertising can help your site achieve your e-marketing objectives by generating interest in your site. Advertising only

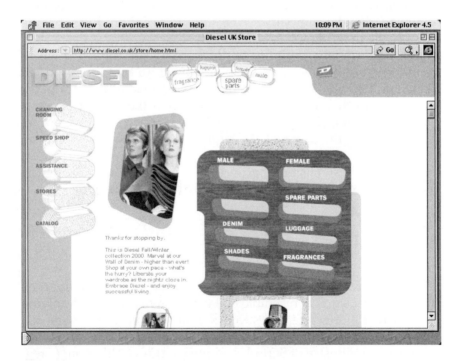

Figure 13.1 Diesel Web site. The Diesel UK site enables you to visit its virtual changing room

works, however, if it is well thought out. Offline advertising campaigns should consolidate not contradict your brand identity. There have been a number of surreal advertising campaigns for Web sites, which have succeeded only in creating awareness for the domain name rather than for what the site actually stands for.

When you have the space you should make people aware of the main reason for coming to your site. One of the easiest ways of doing this is to pose a question and then say you can 'find the answer at www.yoursite.com'. This is a tactic the Royal Mail has used to great effect to promote its Web site. It asks a question such as, 'How can you cut your business overheads by 40 per cent?' and follows it with: 'Find out at www.royalmail.com.' This works because it arouses interest and clearly defines a target audience simultaneously.

It is significant that among those Internet companies that consider advertising important (such as AOL, Yahoo! and Lycos) far more money is spent advertising on traditional media such as TV than on advertising online.

Advertising in the real world can prove more effective than advertising online, but it is often more expensive. If you are investing substantial sums of money into an offline advertising campaign, it is important to remain realistic. According to one US report in Autumn 2000, despite high levels of TV advertising for Web sites, 25 per cent of adults couldn't name one site. (Remember that Internet usage in the US is generally considered to be two years ahead of that in the UK.)

Telecommunications and the Internet

The telephone, via WAP (Wireless Application Protocol) technology, is integrated with the Internet. People no longer need to have access to a PC or an Internet connection to send e-mails and access the Web. WAP telephones have given rise to m-commerce (mobile commerce), whereby users can buy products or services from a Web site via their mobile phone. On account of the limited display size, Internet information is shown in a special format adapted to the display options available on the phone. For this reason, not all Internet services are available. Users can only access specially built 'WAP sites'.

Even if you decide for the moment to ignore the hype surrounding m-commerce, there are many other ways the telephone can be used to enhance your e-marketing activity. These include:

- *Customer support*. Customer support lines (especially freephone numbers) should be included on the e-commerce areas of your site, in order to answer customer queries relating to the order process. Many companies provide a link, represented by a phone icon, to the support line.
- *Follow-up calls*. After e-mailing promotional material a follow-up call can make a big difference and gives you the chance to clear up any points that may have caused confusion.
- *Contact numbers*. A contact telephone number is essential somewhere on your web site, as well as at the foot of your press releases and in your online newsletters. It can also be included in your e-mail signature line.
- *Crisis hotlines*. In the event of a crisis or when you expect a surge of consumer interest you should set up a freephone hotline to prevent an overload of e-mails.
- *Public relations*. The phone is a great networking aid, allowing you to communicate on a personal level with journalists and consumers.

As well as the telephone, there are times when the fax provides valuable e-marketing support. For instance, faxing and e-mailing a press release simultaneously lends your story a greater sense of urgency than it would have if you were to send the release via post. Your fax number should be included alongside your phone number wherever it appears online.

More offline methods

As well as the media and communications channels mentioned above, there are more ways you can supplement your e-marketing with offline media and real world events; these are outlined below.

Ubiquitous URLs

When your Web site is up and running your URL (or Web site address) should be included on all your stationery. After all, the aim is for people to become as familiar (if not more) with your site address as they are with the name of your company. Anything you produce to promote your business should include your domain name: business cards, letterheads, signs, pens, brochures and so on. This will not only help your Web address stay in people's minds, but also enable people to visit your site when they need further information.

Integrated events

The Internet can be used as the focal point for your stand in an exhibition. You can show people your site on a PC on the stand, ask them to subscribe to your e-newsletter and even distribute other e-material. There are also numerous high profile Internet exhibitions and conferences that could provide you with valuable networking opportunities. The search engines Alta Vista, Yahoo! and Lycos are especially helpful for finding out about relevant Internet and trade exhibitions.

Holding a party is one way to mark momentous occasions in the life of your web site (its launch, birthday, makeover and so on). This technique can prove particularly useful in winning over key audiences such as journalists or stakeholders.

Press conferences

The Internet can be used to support press conferences in various ways. Detailed background information and media releases relating to the press conference topic can be included in your online press area prior to the conference. Your media e-mailing list can also be sent e-mails before and after the event to announce and then summarize the conference.

Live footage

Webcams can be used to stream live video footage of an event via your Web site. Microsoft generated massive media coverage and record traffic levels for the UK version of its MSN site (www.msn.co.uk) when it provided live footage of a Madonna concert (see Figure 13.2). The advertising campaign, which interestingly was only targeted at the offline media, provided instructions

Figure 13.2 MSN Web site. Microsoft MSN's live broadcast of a Madonna concert was the first of its kind

on how to view the event, which MSN referred to as 'the best live show ever seen on the Internet'.

Direct mail

Although e-mail is a lot faster and cheaper than using the postal service, there are times when it makes sense to use good old-fashioned 'snail mail' (as it is derogatively referred to by Internet advocates). For one thing, it is much harder for people to ignore something that is sent to them in the post. Also, people tend to be slightly more receptive to unsolicited mail when it is sent in the post than when it is sent electronically. As the quantity of e-mail messages arriving in Internet users' inboxes grows exponentially, more and more people won't read past the subject line of unsolicited e-mails. In fact it is possible to set up e-mail filtering systems that eliminate certain types of e-mail before they even arrive in the recipient's inbox.

You can send out letters, brochures and even CD-ROMs to promote your site. Make sure your letters are as targeted and personal as possible – find out the name of the right person to send your mailings to in advance. As well as for direct mail purposes, you may also need to send out printed press releases and other promotional material to journalists who prefer to be contacted by post than by other methods.

Adding value to real world businesses

A few years ago the question bricks and mortar companies were asking themselves was, 'Can we afford to do business on the Internet?' The question now, however, is, 'Can we afford *not* to do business on the Internet?' As market share is increasingly being eaten up by fast moving Internet start-ups, e-marketing is now seen not only as a way to expand into new markets but also as a means of preserving what a company has already got. However, while it has been acknowledged that online marketing is important for long-term business gain, many have remained sceptical about the short-term benefits. Therefore, while any bricks and mortar company worth its salt now has its own Web site, the Internet is often seen more as a way of promoting a business than as a way of actually *doing* business.

Cisco Systems, the US company responsible for the telecoms hardware that carries traffic across the Internet, has launched various e-business educational programs around the globe. In these programs it talks about the five-stage Internet evolution for any business:

1. The first stage involves using e-mail as a quick, efficient and low-cost alternative to the telephone or postal service.
2. Stage two is when a company moves onto the Web by creating a Web site to act as a 'shop window' for the company and a way of reaching new customers.
3. The third step is e-commerce and the conversion of online traffic into sales, by adding order and payment facilities to the Web site.
4. The next stage occurs when a company decides to use Internet technology to handle e-business areas such as inventory management, accounting, procurement, supplier relationships and staff benefits.

5. The nirvana of this evolutionary model is what Cisco refers to as 'the ecosystem'. This is where the Internet becomes the backbone of the organization, integrating processes and logistics throughout the business.

According to various research findings, the closer a company is to becoming a fully integrated 'ecosystem', the easier it will be to achieve financial success. In late 2000, the Centre for Research in Electronic Commerce at the University of Texas conducted a massive international study, the largest of its kind, into the effects of integrating the Internet with real world business practices. The report, 'E-Business Value Assessment' concluded that by increasing its investment in e-commerce a company increases its chances of financial gain. Michael Dell of Dell Computers, which funded the research, said, 'This study points to a key correlation between how much you integrate the Internet into your business and the financial returns it can achieve.' (Although Dell commissioned the study, the research centre made every effort to ensure the findings were free from any potential commercial bias.)

The conclusions were made after researchers collected and interpreted information from a representative sample of 1200 real world companies of varying sizes in the USA and Europe. Each one of the companies looked at had at least started to utilize the Internet in some form as part of its marketing activity. As David Kirkpatrick, who interpreted the study for *eCompany* magazine has written, 'Of those companies that had seen that an increase in revenue per employee, 40 per cent of all revenue, on average, was flowing in from online sources. Those companies whose revenue per employee had not risen were doing only 10 per cent of their business on the web.' Companies whose gross margins had risen conducted 42 per cent of their business online, compared with only 12 per cent for companies with unmoving margins. All of which goes to show that real world businesses cannot afford to leave the Internet to dot com startups, and must therefore use cyberspace as a way of enhancing their real world activity.

Summary

The important thing to remember when conducting e-marketing activity is that the Internet does not exist in a vacuum. It is practically impossible to market a Web site effectively without utilizing more traditional marketing methods. Equally, it is important for traditional bricks and mortar companies to integrate offline and online marketing efforts. When a company such as Ford (which, for many, is synonymous with the industrial age) embraces online marketing practices and launches new cars via multi-phased e-mail campaigns, it is time to recognize that the Internet constitutes an opportunity, not a threat, for real world businesses.

fourteen

Evaluation

Evaluation is an essential part of any marketing campaign, either online or offline. Measuring results on the Internet, however, is a very different process to tracking results in the real world. As this chapter will explore, the Internet provides marketers with an abundance of methods for quantifying success. Until recently, however, many companies have limited the measurement of their online activity, by focusing on 'hits' or 'unique visits' above all else. This, as we will discover, is a mistake, not only because of the inaccuracy inherent in this form of measurement, but also because of the variety of effective tools at the e-marketer's disposal.

It is, of course, impossible to evaluate the success of Web site or other online activity if you are uncertain about what it should achieve. You need to decide exactly what it is you are measuring if you are to conduct a meaningful evaluation. For instance, proof of increased brand awareness does not necessarily mean that you have achieved your e-marketing objectives if your main aim was to sell x amount of a certain product.

Therefore, before you start the evaluation process, remind yourself exactly why your business is online. Is it to add value to your offline operation, to sell products or services, to provide an extra customer service channel, to expand your business overseas, to cut overheads, or to communicate more effectively with the media? It may be to do a combination of these things or none of them at all, but either way you need to make sure that what you end up measuring relates to your original objectives.

Hits and myths

Although the fact that hits are a very inaccurate way of measuring the number of visitors to a Web site emerged in the late 1990s, many companies persist in judging their site's popularity in terms of their hit count. They will proudly tell advertisers that they receive 10,000 or even a million hits a week in the hope that the advertiser will think that the site receives 10,000 or a million *visitors* a week.

However, one hit does not equal one unique visit. It isn't even a measure of one click-through to a Web page. A hit is a transfer from a Web server to a Web browser. If a page is full of graphics or links, not only will the original click-through to the page register, but also multiple hits will be recorded every time someone clicks on it. This is because every single graphic, no matter how small, registers as one hit as it is sent (via the 'click') from your Web server to the recipient's Web browser. Therefore one unique visit may generate up to a thousand hits as the site user travels around the various pages of a graphic-packed site. A hit does not represent an action made by a visitor to your site. All it represents is an action your *Web server* made while your visitor was at your site.

Hit counters

Hit counters may be the most obvious ways to gauge your Web site's popularity, but they are also one of the least effective. Counters were one of the earliest forms of tracking devices to emerge on the Web and, during the mid-1990s appeared on practically every site that was set up. Their popularity was partly attributable to their simplicity. A Web counter is a very basic program that can be added to just about any Web page. Each time someone clicks on the page, the tiny hit counter program adds another number to its tally. Well, that's the theory. In reality, as we have seen, a hit rarely, if ever, is equal to one unique visit. Furthermore, a poor hit count number is likely to put visitors off your site.

Another reason not to have a hit counter is that it creates an amateurish impression, regardless of the number it displays. Hit counters are extremely simple devices to add to a Web site and as such adorn personal Web sites everywhere (home page greetings such as, 'Welcome visitor 456120' are very common on 'My Pet Fish' type sites). Hit counters are available for free from practically every Internet Service Provider there is, and all it involves is adding a line of HTML to your Web page. It is a much better idea, if you insist on knowing your hit count, to decipher it from your access logs (see below). Hit counters, although well under a decade old, are already past their sell-by date.

Unique visits

As people have become wise to the fact that when they enter a site with an apparent hit count of 22,345 they may only be the fourth visitor, Web sites are increasingly quantifying their success (or at least their popularity) by measuring 'unique visits'.

The way unique visits are measured is via the Web server, which can be used to identify the Internet Protocol (IP) number of a visitor's computer. So, within a designated time frame of, say, 20 minutes, one user can only be registered as one unique visit, no matter how many pages he or she views or how many hits are recorded. However, as this form of visit measurements depends on a fixed time frame, it too falls short of being 100 per cent accurate. For instance, if a user made two unique visits to a Web site within the set time frame, the server would only record it as one visit. Likewise, if someone stayed at a Web site beyond the allocated time, two (or three or four) visits would be registered, even if the user remained at the site the whole time. Furthermore, a user's Internet Protocol number can change every time he or she logs on, which further limits the chances of accuracy. The fact remains however, that 'unique visitor' statistics, although far from perfect, come a lot closer to the mark than hit counts as they do at least provide some indication of your site's popularity.

Access logs and tracking services

If your Web space was provided by a Web hosting company (as opposed to a free service such as GeoCities), your Web site will in all likelihood have its own 'access log'. In simple terms, an access log records all the activity that takes place at your Web site. Every time someone does something at your site (click on a page, make an order, subscribe to your mailing list and so on) your Web server stores the data in the access log.

Access logs provide you with one of the most effective ways of monitoring your Web site activity, because they provide such a comprehensive range of information. This information includes:

- *A host listing.* A host listing provides you with a list of the top 100 or so host computers visiting your site.
- *A domain report.* This report provides you with a list of your visitors' domains.

▪ *Period reports.* These detail all the activity that occurred on your Web site over a set period of time (an hour, day, week, etc).

This information can help you discover not only how often people visit your site, but which areas of the sites are proving most popular. This will provide your e-marketing campaign with some useful guidance as it will tell you what works and what doesn't.

The host listing will help you assess repeat traffic and help you work out why people are coming back to your site (by looking at the areas they return to). Access logs are particularly useful when you are developing or redeveloping your site, as they will provide you with an instant measure of success. You will also get an idea of how long people are staying at your site – if they just pass through or stop there for some lengthy interaction. If you have an e-commerce site (in other words, if you sell your products or services actually on your site) access logs will also help you to work out your conversion rate, that is to say, the number of visitors you are managing to convert into paying customers.

To get hold of your access logs you should get in contact with the company that provides your Web space. If it provides access logs it will either be able to send them to your e-mail account or will tell you to visit a certain Web address to see your logs. However, unless you get excited about computer coding, an access log can be pretty confusing in its raw form. Here is a sample extract from an actual access log:

reqs:	bytes:	%bytes:	host
202:	923:	0.72%:	slip166–172–198–218.tx.us.ibm.net
60:	132:	0.10%:	dial-62.r19.scsumt.infoave.net
55:	673:	0.52%:	max72.kctera.net

This data, in itself, can be quite bewildering, even if you know that the information is taken from a host report, and tells you about the specific 'data transfers' made by the top host computers visiting your site. Therefore, unless you have the time and money to spare to take a crash course in advanced computer programming, you will need to have your access logs translated.

There are a number of services that take the data recorded by your Web hosting company, supplement it with even more 'vital statistics' about your Web site's activity, and then convert it into an easily understandable format. These are useful not only to help direct and assess your e-marketing efforts, but also to gain the interest of your potential advertisers. A condensed version of these reports can also be incorporated within any media packs you send out to journalists and other interested parties. Rather than dividing information into 'host listings', 'domain reports' and 'period reports', it breaks these categories down into a more accessible and user-friendly format. One of the most popular services is available from Web Manage. To give you an idea of the sort of facts and figures such services provide, here is an overview of a Web Manage report, as found at the Web Manage site:

- visitor profile (visitors by continent; top visitor organizations; top visitor countries);
- top requested files;
- top requested file types;
- activity by hour;
- activity by day;
- top visitor browsers;
- technical overview;
- most popular times;
- daily stats;
- weekly stats;
- monthly stats;
- server errors;
- client errors;
- executive summary;
- marketing summary.

The prices of these services vary widely and are often dependent on your site's specific requirements. Here are some of the most widely used fee-based tracking services:

Access Watch (www.accesswatch.com)
Net Gen/Net Analysis (www.netgen.com)
Web Manage (www.webmanage.com)
Web Trends (www.webtrends.com)

Full indexes of fee-based tracking and log analysis programs and services can also be found at Mark Welch's Web site (www.mark welch.com) and at dir.yahoo.com/Business_and_Economy/ Business_to/Business/Communications_and_Networking/Internet _and_World_Wide_Web/Software/internet/World_Wide_Web/Log _Analysis_Tools/.

As well as these advanced fee-based services there are, as we shall see below, a number of free services that provide comprehensive information about your site in exchange for a banner ad being displayed at your site.

Free tracking services

There is a growing number of tracking services and software products available free over the Internet, a lot of which go way beyond providing hit counts. Furthermore, many of these services and products can be customized, so you can tailor them to meet your own specific marketing requirements. Here's a brief overview of some of the most popular free tracking options.

Hitbox (www.hitbox.com)

Hitbox is a tracking service and search engine in one (see Figure 14.1). The search engine indexes sites that use the Hitbox tracking

Figure 14.1 The Hit box Web site. Hit box can provide you with tracking information in exchange for a banner on your site

service and ranks them according to how many hits they receive. Therefore, as well as providing you with comprehensive tracking information this free service also includes your site on its widely used (especially in the business-to-business sector) search engine. The only drawback is that, to use the tracking software you must be willing to incorporate a Hitbox banner ad on your site.

Extreme Tracking (www.extremetracking.co.uk)

Extreme Tracking is a UK-based company that makes free tracking software available for download from the Internet. As well as monitoring hit counts, the Extreme Tracking software can tell you how people are getting to your site (whether via an e-mail or newsletter link, other Web pages, search engines, direct from their browser and so on). If someone reaches your site via a search engine, Extreme Tracking will be able to tell you not only which one but also the exact keywords or phrases the visitor typed in to reach your site. This helps you get a better idea of who your online audience is and can help you improve your search engine rankings by revealing which keywords (and indeed, which search engines) prove most popular.

Super Stats (www.superstats.com)

As with the Extreme Tracking software, Super Stats software helps you identify which search engines and keywords visitors are using to get to your site. Super Stats can also tell you various other personalized facts and figures, such as how long each of your Web pages takes to load on each visitor's Web browser. The free service is supplemented by a more sophisticated fee-based service.

Here are some more similar services:

Hit Watchers (www.hitwatchers.com)
Page Count (www.pagecount.com)
Site Tracker (www.sitetracker.com)

The inadequacy of measuring site visits

As we have seen, hits are a wholly inappropriate and inaccurate way of monitoring e-marketing. Furthermore, while measuring unique visits can lead to a slightly more accurate figure on Web traffic, it doesn't really tell you how successful your site is. As well as the inherent inaccuracies involved in the process, measuring success in terms of visits is not advisable for the reasons discussed below.

Mistake visits
People could arrive at your site and click on the 'back' button as soon as they get there.

Chance visitors
As many as four out of five people visiting a Web site for the first time arrive there via a search engine. As anyone who has used a search engine appreciates, a lot of the sites that come up in search findings are not relevant to whatever it is you are looking for. Furthermore, it often takes a quick visit to the site's home page before realizing that the site is irrelevant for your purpose.

Non-target visitors
Even when people are glad they visited your site, they may not be members of your target audience. For instance, if you are measuring success in terms of the number of customers and potential customers visiting your site it does not mean much if the traffic volume is mainly generated by job-seekers and snooping competitors.

Relationships not eyeballs
As we have discussed elsewhere, e-marketing success is not about the number of 'eyeballs' (people who see your site) your site can generate, but about how effectively it can build and sustain long-term relationships between you and your customers. Visitor figures tell you little, if anything, about how your site is increasing its customers' 'lifetime value'. Remember, in cyberspace it's quality not quantity that counts.

Alternative measures

So, if visitor figures and hit counts are not real measures of success, what is? Although there is no general consensus of opinion, many e-marketers (myself among them) now believe more specific criteria should be looked at. This involves:

- *Analysing media coverage.* Keeping track of your site's profile in the online and offline media is essential, in order to gauge the awareness of your Web brand.
- *Monitoring newsgroups and mailing list discussion groups.* One of the great (although sometimes scary) things about the Internet is that everyone has an equal say. This means you can find out what consumers *really* think of your site by looking out for mentions in interactive online forums such as newsgroups and mailing list discussion groups.
- *Sales.* If you are selling products or services directly from your site, the best measure of success is your sales figures. By looking out for any fluctuations in your sales statistics, you will be able to steer your e-marketing activity in the right direction.
- *Actions.* Actions speak louder than hit counts on the Internet, so always look out for any positive actions visitors have made at your site. Monitor how many people subscribe to your e-newsletter, fill in forms, purchase products and participate in your chat area or newsgroup (if you have one).
- *Search engine rankings.* Once you have submitted your site to all the major search engines, you should check your search position on a regular basis using a free service such as Website-Rank (www.Website-rank.com) or My Rank (www.myrank.com). You could also use downloadable rank checking software such as Web Position (www.webposition.com).
- *Feedback.* One of the most obvious ways to monitor your e-marketing success is to ask for feedback from your site visitors. You can do this either via e-mail or through a form at your site. Internet responses have proved to be more honest than any other form of contact, and as such will give you a more accurate picture of how people view your site than more traditional market research methods.
- *Monitor associated sites.* Any sites you are associated with (through affiliate schemes, link partnerships, sponsorships, advertising deals or any other means) should be monitored to help you to decide whether the association should continue.
- *Monitor competitors' sites.* By keeping track of your competition (through search engines, media coverage, newsgroup postings, etc) you will be able to get a better idea of your own market share.

Using search engines

If you want to monitor the impact of your e-marketing activity beyond your Web site (and you should), you will need to use search engines on a regular basis. Search engines will not only help you to keep track of your own profile, but also that of your competition. When searching the Web for references to your company or Web site remember not to limit searches to just the company itself. After all, keyword searches based on the words 'Bill Gates' or 'Richard Branson' would come up with quite different matches to searches based on the words 'Microsoft' or 'Virgin'.

Obviously you cannot be expected to check the search engines every day, so it may prove helpful to use a free automated search engine tracking service such as Net Mind (www.netmind.com). This service monitors any changes made to any of the major search engines and, once your have provided it with the keywords or phrases you want to cover, will e-mail you every time a relevant new addition occurs.

In addition to concentrating on search engines with Web site indexes such as Yahoo! (www.yahoo.com), Excite (www.excite.com – co.uk) and Lycos (www.lycos.com) you should also visit newsgroups and mailing list search engines such as Deja News (www.deja.com) and Liszt (www.liszt.com).

Link monitoring

As mentioned above, one way to keep track of your site's marketing activity is to monitor sites with which you have reciprocal links. However, owing to the fact that anyone can incorporate a link to your site without your knowledge, you should also keep track of sites that are linking to you without a link back.

The way to discover all the Web sites including a link to your site is to visit a search engine that enables you to conduct 'link searches'. AltaVista (www.altavista.com – .co.uk), Hotbot (www.hotbot.com) and Infoseek (www.infoseek.com) all provide this facility.

To find links using AltaVista, simply log on to the AltaVista site and type in 'Link:' in the search box followed by your Web site address, such as: link: www.mysite.com, or even: link:mysite.com. To check links from your own site you will need to use the host: command as well, so the full entry into the search box would read: link: www.mysite.com – host:www.mysite.com.

To search all the search engines with link search facilities at once, visit the link meta-search site, Link Popularity (www.linkpopularity.com) and fill in its brief submission form.

Online clipping services

Owing to the sheer size of the Web, and the phenomenal speed with which it moves, it can be virtually impossible to keep track of when and where your company is mentioned. If you are attempting to gain media coverage, however, online clipping services can help you monitor both the online and offline media for mentions of your company or Web site.

Online clipping services monitor not only Web sites but also e-mail newsletters, e-zines, Usenet newsgroups and discussion boards. Some services even scour peer-to-peer networks such as Freenet, and can find references to your company in e-mails and other computer-based documents.

The way they work is simple. You give them certain keywords (your Web site address, company name, key members of staff, etc) and the tracking firm uses sophisticated and expensive software to track the Internet for your keywords. Most then provide you with a report of where they were mentioned and also an evaluation of how significant each matching was.

Not only will these services be able to track positive coverage when you are carrying out a publicity blitz, but they can also be used to monitor any negative mentions on the Web or in discussion groups. The costs of these services varies between around \$100/£60 and \$400/£250 per month. Below are some of the most popular services.

News Tracker (www.excite.com)

NewsTracker is a clipping service offered by the major search engine, Excite. Although it is limited to the Web, News Tracker is a reliable and cost-effective service that is proving increasingly popular.

EWatch (www.eWatch.com – .co.uk)

At the other end of the scale is eWatch (see Figure 14.2), a service of PR Newswire that is particularly popular among companies

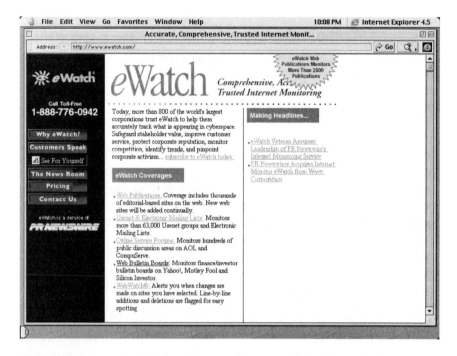

Figure 14.2 E-watch Web site. PR Newswire's E-watch service can help you track negative publicity

wishing to keep track of references in online publications as well as negative or libellous comments made on the net. The service has helped companies uncover stock scams and detect misinformation online.

Durrants (www.durrants.co.uk)

Durrants is one of the UK's largest press cutting agencies, and a firm favourite among PR consultancies. Alongside its print and broadcast services it now also offers electronic monitoring.

Cyber Alert (www.cyberalert.com)

Cyber Alert draws on both technology and human resources to conduct searches on 'feeder sites' (any searchable Web-based resource). Once you have provided sets of keywords to search for, the service collects, sorts and edits its search findings before saving them in an 'in box' that can be accessed by logging on to the Web site. The difference with Cyber Alert is that, unlike many other online clipping services, it doesn't limit its searches to Web sites; it can even search Web-based newsgroups for relevant messages.

Cyber Check (www.cybercheck.com)

As with Cyber Alert, Cyber Check collects newsgroup postings as well. Basically, you can choose either to pay from the Web Check service (which only monitors Web sites) or the Forum Check service (which monitors over 150,000 online forums), or to have both services run at the same time.

Other services include:

BMC News (www.bmcnews.com)
Cyber Scan (www.cyberscan.com)
Web Clipping (www.webclipping.com)
Cyber Clipping (www.cyberclipping.com)
Net Currents (www.netcurrents.com)

For full listings of clipping services (both on the Internet and offline) visit dir.yahoo.com/Business_and_Economy/Business_ to_Business/Corporate_Services/Public_Relations/Clipping_and_ Monitoring_Services/.

Encouraging feedback

The ultimate way to evaluate your e-marketing efforts is to encourage feedback from your visitors themselves. By turning your Web site into a two-way communication tool, you will be able to gauge the opinion of your visitors every step of the way. This will also help you to build brand loyalty by making people feel a valued part of the process.

On the Internet there is a considerable overlap between marketing evaluation and customer research. In many ways they are one and the same thing. Finding out what the customer wants is, after all, a very similar process to discovering what the customer thinks about your company or Web site. Both activities involve engaging in some form of dialogue or conversation with your online audience. Outlined below are some of the ways you can measure marketing success through talking to and listening to your online customers.

Incorporate response forms on your site

Provided you offer a meaningful incentive to fill them in, interactive forms can be very useful evaluation tools. Furthermore, adding questionnaire forms to your site is a lot simpler than putting together an order form. If you use a WYSIWYG ('What You See Is What You Get') Web design program it can be as simple as cutting and pasting a form template.

When you are putting together a question and answer form, think of the questions that are most likely going to provoke a direct and honest response. Questions such as 'Where are we going wrong?' and 'Where are we going right?' indicate to a site visitor that you are willing to accept no-holds-barred answers.

Use your own online forums

By creating a chat room, bulletin board or mailing list discussion group you have your very own focus group at your disposal, with which to test out new ideas and evaluate old ones. Ministry of Sound (www.ministryofsound.com) is one Web site that uses its online forums to evaluate its marketing successes and failures. The 'VIP' moderated chat room often forms the testing ground for the Ministry of Sound's new online and offline projects.

Amazon.com is another company that uses its online communities for evaluative purposes. When the company was toying with the idea of variable pricing, it tested out the idea on its wide range of DVDs. The company then monitored its DVD Talk chat forum to gauge the response. Quickly realizing that the variable pricing idea was a wholly unpopular one, Amazon.com ceased its pricing experiment.

Incorporate a guest book

Guest books are a very simple but surprisingly effective feedback mechanism, which can be added to just about any site. As with real world guest books, they give visitors a free rein to say whatever they like about their experience at your site. Freecode (www.freecode.com) offers a range of free guest book packages that you can add to your Web pages.

Use your mailing list

Generally speaking, the people who choose to subscribe to your online mailing list are also the people who are most willing to provide you with feedback. If you send out an electronic newsletter, you can ask subscribers for comment on both the newsletter and your site. Wilson Web's Web Marketing Today newsletter regularly asks subscribers for their opinion on new features by putting decisions to a vote (see www.webmarketingtoday.com).

As well as incorporating evaluation questions within your newsletter you could also send out separate e-mails asking for comment on past, present and future online activity. In this case, however, it is better to cut down your subscriber list to a sample cross-section. This will enable you to personalize each message, and therefore guarantee a better response than if you sent out a questionnaire as a mass mailing.

Ongoing evaluation

In the real world, marketing practitioners tend to use evaluation techniques as a means of assessing a campaign's success once it has been completed. Almost without exception, evaluation is something that takes place after the event. A PR or advertising campaign will be implemented within a designated timescale of, say, six months and then at the end of that set period, the people who put the campaign together will evaluate its success. Typically, they put their findings down on paper in the form of a 'Campaign Report' or an 'Evaluative Overview' that will provide a focus for future campaigns.

On the Internet, however, there is little time for hindsight. Whereas in the real world a company is one step removed from the media it uses to promote its products or service, on the Internet the company, via its Web site, *becomes* the medium. There is no time for a contemplative pause between promotional campaigns because your Web site constitutes in itself one long, ongoing marketing campaign. Therefore, just as the Internet blurs the real world boundaries of time and geography, it also gets rid of the dividing lines between the different stages and components of marketing activity. As a result of this, evaluation must become an ongoing process and be seen as something that takes place throughout every stage of your e-marketing campaign.

Summary

Evaluation is an essential part of practically all online activity. It must be remembered, however, that measuring results is not an end in itself. Results need to be responded to and acted upon if marketing goals are to be met. As the Internet is an ever-changing medium, evaluation is an ongoing process and results are not set in stone.

Although it is unlikely that you will be able to get everything right all the time, that may not ultimately be the point. By involving your audience in the evaluation process, rather than depending solely on technology, you will be embracing the Internet on its own interactive terms. Furthermore, this means the evaluation process itself can help strengthen the bond between your site and its visitors, so even if some of your marketing tactics end up heading in the wrong direction, your overall strategy will always remain on course.

A guide to **HTML and meta-tags**

Whether you decide to create your web site yourself or get someone else to do it for you, a solid understanding of HTML (HyperText Mark-up Language) will prove invaluable for your e-marketing efforts. Knowing all the main HTML commands will enable you to amend and adjust your web site at no extra cost. This can help you not only to keep your content fresh, but also to improve your ranking on the major search engines. Furthermore, HTML commands can help you in other areas of e-marketing beyond your web site. An HTML formatted newsletter, for instance, can be a lot more effective than one that has been constructed using Word or Office software. Even if you have web building software such as Dreamweaver or Microsoft Front Page, which converts the HTML for you, a basic knowledge of HTML will enable you to use these programs to greater effect. Indeed many of the software packages allow you to add HTML tags directly.

HTML defined

HTML is the DNA of the Internet. It is a type of word-processing language deployed by Internet users to build and design pages that can be uploaded onto the web. HTML tells the web browser how the text, graphics and links of a web page should be displayed. It does this through commands that are enclosed in chevron brackets to form tags.

To understand HTML better, it is useful to look at what the term means. *Hypertext*, as you may or may not be aware, is defined as text that incorporates links within it. *Mark-up Language* is a term coined by computer programmers which, in plain English, simply means a way of incorporating information about a document into the document itself. Normally, as in the case of HTML, this is done by using tag commands. To see what HTML looks like log onto any web page then click on 'View' followed by 'Page Source'.

The essential facts about HTML

Unlike other languages, HTML is thoroughly consistent. Once you have come to terms with its essential characteristics you will realize that there are rarely any exceptions. The main facts you need to take on board about HTML are as follows:

- *HTML is a sequence of tags*. As briefly explained above, HTML instructions are provided in pieces of text called tags.
- *HTML works in pairs*. Most HTML commands consist of pairs in order to indicate where each instruction starts and finishes. For instance, if you want a piece of text displayed as **bold**, you would place it between the commands <B> and </B>. (The back slash effectively means 'end' or 'off'.)
- *Capital letters are always used for HTML commands*. This is primarily to distinguish them from the rest of the text.
- *HTML is invisible*. As HTML tags work behind the scenes of a web site, they remain invisible to the end user.
- *HTML appears differently on different browsers*. Different web browsers display HTML formatted text in different ways. You will need to check what each web page looks like on the various types of browsers before you upload your site (or other HTML-based document) onto the Internet.

The main HTML tags

Although most people are intimidated by the idea of learning HTML it is surprisingly easy to get to grips with. The reason for this is that as the main HTML tags occur over and over again, you only need to know a few commands to put an HTML formatted web page together.

The commands that will prove the most useful are as follows:

<HTML></HTML> These tags surround the entire document and
   identify the document as HTML.
<HEAD></HEAD> These tags are put on either site of the title tags at
   the start of an HTML document.
<TITLE></TITLE> The title tags surround a short description of the
   document. This description is for your purposes only and is not seen
   on the screen.
<BODY></BODY> These tags surround everything that isn't included
   within the <HEAD></HEAD> commands at the top of the document.
<H1></H1> The first heading at the top of a document is surrounded
   by the <H1> and </H1> tags. Subsequent heading tags are given
   higher numbers.
<I></I>*Text to be displayed in italics is enclosed by these tags.*
<B></B>**The bold tags surround text to be displayed in bold.**
<HR>Standing for horizontal rule, this single tag displays a horizontal
   line that is good for separating sections of documents.
<P></P> These tags indicate the start and finish of a paragraph.
<A></A> Underlined text to indicate a hypertext link goes between
   these anchor tags. The letters HREF (standing for hypertext
   reference) follow the first A. Here is an example: <A HREF=
   "http://www.website.com"> web site </A>
<IMRG SRC> This is a single tag that instructs the browser to put an
   image on the web site. A filename is always included within the
   brackets to tell the browser where the image can be found. For
   instance, <IMG SRC = "Bud Pic.gif">.

These tags will enable you to make some sense of the HTML coding
underlying web pages. They will certainly help you understand
how the World Wide Web jigsaw is pieced together.

The anatomy of an HTML document

HTML documents are structured around the meta-tags (see below)
that help search engines analyse your site. Generally, all HTML documents fit within the following format:

<HTML>
<HEAD><TITLE> (the title of the web page goes here) </TITLE>
   </HEAD>

```
<BODY> (the bulk of the document fits in here)</BODY>
</HTML>
```

There are therefore two essential parts of an HTML document: the head section and the body section. The head section commands the web browser to display information on the top bar of a window (as it appears on the screen), while the body section constitutes the web page itself.

Creating HTML documents

An HTML document is a plain text document that has HTML instructions incorporated within it. You can create an HTML document by using a web building tool (which will hide some of the scarier details of HTML) or a word-processing program. Most word-processing software packages now accommodate HTML and have a 'Save as HTML' option.

Whichever way you decide to create your HTML file you will need to see how it will eventually look when it's up on the web. To do this you will need to follow these instructions:

- Save your document to disc (make sure you add the .htm suffix to your file name).
- Go into your web browser.
- Choose the commands 'File' then 'Open' to access the saved document. The document will then appear as it will when it is uploaded onto the web.

Within the <BODY></BODY> tags you place your text and HTML instructions. Typically, the body section starts off with a heading placed between the <H1> and </H1> tags. After the heading you can then write your text, which can be split into paragraphs by using the paragraph <P> tag. Other format tags can be added to add life to your document. The commands for using italics and bold and for adding horizontal rules and images have already been mentioned. Some of the other 'format tags' are outlined below.

Lists

HTML enables you to incorporate two main types of list into your web documents: bulleted and ordered.

Bulleted lists. lists are enclosed within the <UL> and </UL> commands. You can then use <LI> to indicate the start of each item.

Ordered lists. Ordered (or numbered) lists work in much the same way except the <UL> tags are exchanged for the commands <OL> and </OL>. Placed within these commands the <LI> tag will display numbers instead of bullet points (the browser automatically places the numbers in sequence).

Here's an example of how to format an ordered list (followed by the same list as it would appear on a web browser):

<OL> The top three web design disasters:

<LI> Information overload
<LI> Brochureware
<LI> Style over substance
<OL>

The top three web design disasters:

1. Information overload
2. Brochureware
3. Style over substance

Colours

To add a background colour you will need to incorporate the additional command BGCOLOR as well as specify the colour you want within the body tags, such as:

<BODY BGCOLOR = "red">

If you then wanted to change the colour of the text from black to white you would need to follow this command with another body tag:

<BODY TEXT = "white">

Likewise, to change the colour of link commands you use the following command:

<BODY LINK = "green">

Meta-tags

Meta-tags are the most important HTML commands for the Internet marketer to get right, because they are analysed by search engine 'robots' as they trawl through the web. If you don't your site could be left in the depths of cyberspace, making effective use of meta-tags will ensure you get a good search engine ranking.

Like other HTML tags, meta commands remain invisible to the person visiting your site. Their purpose is to tell search engines and other web tools about the content of your site. Without meta-tags search engine programs will be unable to prioritize site content and therefore judge every single word of text between all your HTML commands as being of equal importance. That means every 'so', 'if' and 'but' in your site will be counted as a keyword. By using meta-tags you can strip your site down to its bare essentials and eliminate superfluous information.

There are two main types of meta-tag: the description tag and the keyword tag.

The description meta-tag

Description meta-tags are used to describe your web site as a whole, as well as each individual page. Descriptions placed within meta-tags should be between 15 and 30 words long. Here's an example of what a META description tag looks like:

> <META name = "description" content = "A popular organic food and drink web site providing health and recipe information alongside a wide range of tasty products.">

This description tag (for The Organic Shop) could then be placed under the title of the site on search engines. This often provides more information than the first 20 or so words of the main text ('Hi, welcome to our site...', etc) which would otherwise be included. It is worth taking some time in coming up with a good meta description because it can then be recycled for use on search engine submission forms.

The keywords meta-tag

The keywords meta-tag enables you to list keywords which search engines can match with the words their users type in. Therefore, when you are coming up with your list you should try and think about the words and phrases members of your target audience would be likely to type in to find a site like yours. The keywords meta-tag normally follows the description tag within the head section, such as:

```
<Head>
<Title> The Organic Shop Home Page </Title>
<META name = 'description" content = "A popular food and drink
    web site providing health and recipe information alongside a wide
    range of tasty products.">
<META name = "keywords" content = "organic, food, drink,
    vegetables, recipes, health, wine, fruit, juice, diet, information,
    meat, groceries">
</Head>
```

Although meta-tags are among the most important HTML commands, many web designers ignore them as they do not affect the appearances of your site. This is a big mistake. Even if you are prepared to continually submit your site to every major search engine yourself, if you miss out your meta-tags you may be wasting your time. As competition to be included on search engines gets ever more intense, so the major search sites are starting to discriminate against sites without meta-tags in much the same way as they discriminate against sites that don't have a domain name.

For a complete list of HTML tags take a look at Kevin Werbach's Guide to HTML (www.werbach.com/barebones). If you are after more information on how meta-tags can be used to improve your search engine ranking, visit Search Engine Watch (www.searchenginewatch.com).

E-marketing
dictionary

ADSL Asymmetric Digital Subscriber Line. A high speed, high *bandwidth* telephone line.

address book A directory in a web browser where you can store and manage e-mail addresses.

article The name given to a single message posted to a newsgroup.

attachment A file added to an e-mail to be sent via the e-mail system.

audience Refers to each individual section of your online public. Each business has various audiences (customers, investors, journalists, etc).

B2B Business-to-business.

B2C Business-to-consumer.

Bps Bits per second. The speed by which modems are measured.

B-web Business web. The term 'b-web' was first coined by the US Internet journalist and consultant Don Tapscott to refer to the information age's 'primary business unit, in which groups of firms come together over the Internet. While each company retains its identity, the companies function together, creating more wealth than they could ever hope to create individually'.

bandwidth The capacity of fibre optic cables that carry information. The higher the bandwidth, the faster information will pass through a cable.

banner ad An online advertisement in the form of a band of text and graphics. Banner ads generally contain a hypertext link to the advertiser's site.

banner views Refers to the number of times a banner has been viewed.

Tim Berners Lee Conceived the web in 1989 as a tool for sharing information via his invention of HTML. Now he is the director of the World Wide Web Consortium (W3C).

Jeff Bezos Founder and CEO of Amazon.com.

binaries Files attached to newsgroup articles, usually in the form of images or zip files.

biometrics Voice and fingerprint recognition.

Boolean search A search allowing the inclusion or exclusion of documents containing certain words through the use of operators such as AND, NOT and OR.

bookmark A bookmark is a software tool that automatically loads the page it refers to.

bricks and clicks Refers to an integrated offline/online approach.

bricks and mortar A phrase used to evoke the 'real world'.

bricolage Claude Levi-Strauss, the French anthropologist, refers to *bricolage* as the act of creating things from whatever is lying around. Many people use the term to describe the opportunistic way in which the web is put together.

broadband High bandwidth technology that is revolutionizing the way the Internet is used by businesses and consumers.

browser Software that allows you to access the Internet and World Wide Web. Internet Explorer and Netscape Navigator are the most commonly used browsers.

bulletin board Software that provides an e-mail database where people can access and leave messages.

C2C Consumer-to-consumer.

CPA Cost per action. A pricing model for online advertising based on the number of times an Internet user clicks on a banner ad that is linked to your web site.

CPM Cost per thousand impressions. Another pricing model for online advertising (the M is the Roman numeral for 1000).

cache A small memory bank inside an Internet user's computer. Each time you visit web sites on the Internet, the cache stores all the images and text from those sites. This speeds up the download time when users revisit a site.

cancel option Useful in mail and newsgroup systems. Allows you to delete a message before or just after posting an e-mail message or newsgroup article.

Steve Case CEO of AOL.

chat system Enables users to have an interactive, typed conversation. Chat systems build an online network of people who interact not just with the web page but with other users as well.

clicks and mortar See *bricks and clicks*.

click through This refers to the act of clicking on a link to be transported to another site. The phrase is most commonly used in the context of banner advertising.

click through rate (CTR) The percentage of click throughs to banner views.

community A group of Internet users with a shared interest or concept who interact with each other in news groups, mailing-list discussion groups and other online interactive forums.

concept search A search for documents related conceptually to a word, rather than specifically containing the word itself.

content services Sites dedicated to a particular topic.

conversion rate The percentage of shoppers in an online store who actually make a purchase.

cookies Small files that recognize repeat users of a web site.

corporate portals Web sites for employees.

crawler A type of search engine 'robot'.

cross-posting The act of posting the same messages into several different news or discussion groups simultaneously.

cyberspace Term originally coined in the sci-fi novels of William Burroughs, referring to the online world and its communication networks and evoking its intangible sense of space.

DSL/Cable Modems High-speed computer modems for use with a cable or phone network.

digital ink Changeable electronically charged ink particles.

disintermediation Refers to the fact that the Internet enables companies to bypass intermediaries such as journalists and editors to communicate directly with their audience.

distribution list A list of e-mail addresses given one collective title. You can send a message to all the addresses simultaneously by referring to the list title.

domain name The officially registered web site address of your site.

dot bam Dot 'bricks and mortar'. A real world business with a strong web presence.

dot com Used to refer to a company based exclusively online.

download The term used to describe the transfer of a computer file from a server to a PC.

e-business The catchall term referring to the business world online. It also signifies an individual online business or company.

e-commerce Refers to business transactions over the Internet.

e-mail Electronic mail. A message sent across the Internet, or the act of transferring messages between computers, mobile phones or other communications attached to the Internet.

e-mail system The collective e-mail software systems that allow you to create, send and receive e-mail messages.

e-mailing list A collection of e-mail addresses.

e-media relationships The practice of building relationships with editors and journalists via the Internet, especially when they work for the e-media.

e-media release An online, interactive press release sent via the e-mail system.

encryption The process of converting data into a coded form.

e-tailing The selling of retail goods on the World Wide Web.

e-TV Interactive television, accessed via a computer or a TV set.

e-zines Online interactive magazines that only exist on the Internet.

emoticons Common symbols used in e-mail and news group messages to denote particular emotions by resembling faces on their side. :-) therefore indicates happiness (a smiley face), while :-(conveys happiness (an unhappy face). The word 'emoticon' is a hybrid of 'emotion' and 'icon'.

FTP File Transfer Protocol This is the standard method of uploading content from your computer to your server.

filter Software This can discriminate between types of incoming and out-going e-mail messages.

flame A 'heated' and hostile message posted in a newsgroup, usually in response to 'spam'; also, the act of posting such a message.

form A means of collecting data on web pages, using text boxes, radio buttons and other facilities. Forms are used as a way of making sites more interactive as well as for sales and marketing purposes.

forums Newsgroups, mailing-list discussion groups, chat rooms and other online areas that allow you to read, post and respond to messages.

freeware Free software programs.

full-text index An index consisting of every single word of every document catalogued.

fuzzy search A search that will find matches even when words are only partially spelled or misspelled.

Bill Gates Microsoft Chairman. Although slow to appreciate the importance of the Internet, Gates has converted Microsoft into a company aiming to write the code for the next generation of net-compatible devices.

GIF Graphic Information File. Used on the Internet to display files that contain graphic images.

groupware A set of technology tools enabling businesses to share software.

Guerrilla marketing Refers to any extreme or outlandish attempt to generate publicity, either online or offline.

history list A record of visited web pages you can access through your browser. It can help you find sites you haven't been able to bookmark.

hits A hit is a transfer from a server to a browser. Each time a browser transfers a text page that has no graphics, that represents one hit. If the page has a graphic inside it, that's two hits. If it has two graphics that's three hits, and so on. Hits therefore do not provide an accurate measurement of the number of times your web site has been visited.

hit counters Software that records hits.

home page The first and or main page on a web site.

host A company that holds your site on its server.

host computer This simply refers to a computer connected to the Internet.

HTML Hypertext Mark-up Language. A computer code used to build and develop web pages.

hyperlinks See *hypertext links*.

hypertext links Generally found on web pages (although they can be used in e-mail messages), they link onto HTML pages and documents.

hypertime Refers to the fast moving pace of the Internet, as well as the decentralized nature of online time.

index The searchable catalogue of documents created by search engine software.

information overload The situation of having so much information on your site as to bore or intimidate your customer.

Internet The global network of computers accessed with the aid of a modem. The Internet includes web sites, e-mail, newsgroups and other forums. This is a public network, though many of the computers connected to it are also part of *Intranets*. It uses the Internet Protocol (IP) as a communication standard.

intranet Internal, private computer networks using Internet technology to allow communication between individuals within organizations.

IRC Internet Relay Chat (see *chat*).

ISP Internet Service Provider. A firm that provides Internet services such as e-mail and web hosting facilities.

itchy finger syndrome A slang reference to the Internet users' hunger for interactivity.

java Web programming language that works on any computing platform.

junk mail See *spam*.

keywords Words used by search engines to help find and register sites.

keyword search A search for documents containing one or more words that are specified by a search engine user.

kill file An instruction used in a newsgroup by your newsreader to skip particular articles, according to criteria you specify.

links Text or graphic icons that move you to different web pages or sites. Links are activated by clicking them with a mouse.

list server Software that runs a mailing list.

log on/off To access/leave the Internet.

lower-level domain The main part of the domain name. For most e-business sites this is usually the company or brand name.

lurk To read messages in newsgroups or mailing list discussion groups, but not post anything yourself.

m-commerce Mobile commerce. E-commerce via mobile phones using WAP and other technologies.

Scott McNealy Chairman and CEO, Sun Microsystems. Was instrumental in the shaping of the Internet.

mail server A remote computer (usually your ISP) enabling you to send and receive e-mails.

meta-tags The keyword and description commands used in your web page code to help search engines index your web site.

micropayments Internet transactions for very small amounts.

Modem Modulator/demodulator. This is an internal or external piece of hardware plugged into your PC or Mac. It links into a phone socket enabling computer-based information to be transmitted over a phone network.

moderator Someone in charge of a newsgroup, mailing-list discussion group or similar forum. The moderator censors any unwelcome messages.

multi-phased medium A medium, such as the Internet, which can be used in different means for different ends.

navigation The way a visitor travels around, or is directed around a web site, via links.

net Shorthand for Internet.

net-head Internet-obsessed individual.

netiquette The etiquette of the Internet. It is used mainly in the context of e-mail and newsgroup communication.

newbie Slang term for a new newsgroup member.

news reader Software enabling you to search, read, post and arrange newsgroup messages.

newsgroups Collectively referred to as the 'Usenet', newsgroups are online discussion areas centred on a subject of common interest. People post messages to the groups, which all the other members can read. There are over 40,000 active newsgroups on the Internet covering topics as diverse as Social Welfare Reform and South Park.

niche A narrow but unified market or audience segment. The Internet is particularly suited to niche markets and audiences.

NNTP Network News Transport Protocol. In newsgroups NNTP is the method by which newsreader software communicates with news servers across the Internet.

offline Used to denote any activity or situation that does not involve being connected to the Internet.

online The state of being connected via a modem to the Internet.

operating system Software stored in a computer that controls hardware components and the processes that run on them.

P2P Peer-to-peer. Referring to technology that allows internet users to download compressed files from other users. Can also stand for 'path to profitability', which investors look for in new internet start-ups.

phrase search A search for documents containing an exact sentence or phrase specified by a search engine user.

plaintext Text that is encoded and contains no layout information; non-HTML text.

portal As in the real world, a portal on the Internet grants you access to other places.

post The act of sending an article to a newsgroup.

precision The degree to which a search engine lists documents matching a query. The more matching documents that are listed, the higher the precision.

pure brands E-brands are often referred to as pure brands because they are unburdened by real world constraints, such as their geographic location.

rank A search engine position.

real world Everything outside the Internet.

recall Related to precision, this is the degree to which a search engine returns all the matching documents in a collection.

refresh The act of reloading a web site page or site.

robot A tool used by search engines to find and examine web sites.

run of site (ROS) Refers to displaying a banner ad throughout a web site or a banner network with no targeting by keyword or site category.

SSL Secure Sockets Layer. The main type of secure server used to take orders online and to transfer sensitive information.

search engine A site that enables you to conduct a keyword search of indexed information on its database. Also refers to the software used in this process.

secure server Hardware and software that secure e-commerce credit card transactions so there is no risk of people gaining access to credit card details online.

signature (file) Information appended to the end of a message that identifies the sender's details. You only need to write a signature file once and you can then attach it to your e-mails as often as you like.

silver surfers Mature Internet users.

smiley see *emoticon*.

snail mail Net-head term for the real world postal service.

snooze news Company 'news' that will not interest journalists or editors.

spam Junk mail on the Internet, normally in the form of unsolicited and unwelcome e-mail messages. The term is used most frequently in the context of newsgroups referring to the same article being posted repeatedly to different newsgroups. The term comes from the famous Monty Python 'Spam, Spam, Spam' sketch where Spam is served with everything.

spider A type of search engine 'robot'.

stemming The ability for a search to include the 'stem' of words.

system administrator Someone responsible for the management of an e-mail system.

sysop Systems operator. See *moderator*.

thread An ongoing newsgroup topic.

top-level domain The concluding part of a domain name, such as the .com or .co.uk suffixes.

traffic The number of people visiting your site.

trolling The act of posting a newsgroup article with the deliberate intent of provoking a heated or 'flamed' response.

URL Uniform Resource Locator. A full web address, for example: http://www.yac.com.

usenet The system that distributes newsgroups. Also the collective term for newsgroups.

visitors The people who come to your web site.

WAP Wireless Application Protocol. The mobile equivalent of HTML.

Web master Someone in charge of a Web site.

Web page A single document stored at a Web site. A single Web browser window displays a single web page at a time.

Web rings Collections or communities of different Web sites and pages.

Web site A collection of web pages.

World Wide Web/Web The World Wide Web does not mean the Internet. The World Wide Web is, in fact, a software system running across the Internet. It consists of (literally) billions of web pages, usually containing text, images and HTML links.

Yahoo! The world's most popular search engine.

index

RAM (Random Access
    Memory)   13
'realistic' objectives   8
reality sites   205–06
reassurance schemes   131
reciprocal links   77–81
registration with search engines
    67–72
repeat traffic   86–90, 136–37
reputations, importance of
    154–55
research   17–35
    automated response   32–33
    competitor   29–31
    e-mail   26–28
    information collection   33
    media   182–83
    newsgroups   28–29
    primary research   25–26
    search engines   18–25
    useful sites   34
    via own site   31–32
response forms *see* forms
returns policy   130

Savvy Search   24
search commands   21–22
Search Engine Watch   34
search engines   18–25, 61–75
    advertising on   174–75
    cheating   72–73, 197
    evaluating technique   73–74,
        224
    preparation   61–67
    registering   67–72
search facilities   56
secondary research sites   34
security issues   129–31, 134
segmented Web sites   12
selling on the Web   119–31
    auctioning   128–29
    price pressure   126–27

processing orders   121–22
security issues   129–31
software   122–26
services, online selling of   120
shared purpose of online
    communities   153–54
Shop Site   124–25
shopping-cart (shop in a box)
    systems   121–22, 122–26
    software   14, 43–44
'signature lines'   111–12
'simplicity' rule   50, 134
site maps   51
site visit measurement
    221–22
Slice   194
SMART objectives   7–8
software
    online selling   120
    Web design   14, 42–44
space, buying advertising
    172–74
spam   94–96
spam indexing   73
'specific' objectives   8
'speed marketing' characteristic
    2
sponsorships   170–71
SSL (Secure Socket Layer)
    servers   129, 130
Stains SOS (Persil)   58
strategies   9–10
subcontractors   137
submission programs   70
subscriber lists   171–72
subscribers, winning over
    potential   109–10
Super Stats   221
superstitials   170
survey findings, publicizing
    181
systems operators   112–13

Other E-Business titles published by Kogan Page include:

Advertising on the Internet, 2nd edn (2001) Steven Armstrong
Brand Building on the Internet (2001) Martin Lindström and
   Tim Frank Andersen
Clicks, Bricks and Brands (2001) Martin Lindström
Doing Business on the Internet, 3rd edn (1999) Simon Collin
E-Business Essentials (2001) Matt Haig
E-Business Start-up Guide (2000) Philip Treleaven
E-PR: The Essential Guide to Online Public Relations (2000) Matt Haig
E-Business for the Small Business: Making profit from the Internet
   (2001) John G Fisher
Guide to Web Marketing (2000) Judy Davis

The above titles are available from all good bookshops or direct
from the publishers. To obtain more information, please contact the
publishers at the address below:

Kogan Page
120 Pentonville Road
London N1 9JN
Tel: (020) 7278 0433
Fax: (020) 7837 6348
www.kogan-page.co.uk

Visit Kogan Page on-line

Comprehensive information on
Kogan Page titles

Features include

- complete catalogue listings,
  including book reviews and
  descriptions

- special monthly promotions

- information on NEW titles and
  BESTSELLING titles

- a secure shopping basket facility
  for on-line ordering

PLUS everything you need to know
about KOGAN PAGE

http://www.kogan-page.co.uk